IT'S A GREAT LIFE IF YOU
DON'T
WEAKEN

THE POWER OF NEXT

JERRY X SHEA

WARNING-DISCLAIMER

Published by: Icon Holdings, Inc. P.O. Box 1445, Cambria, CA 93428

www.JerryXShea.com

Copyright 2013 by Jerry X Shea

Library of Congress Control Number 2012913107

Shea, Jerry X 1943 -

It's A Great Life If You Don't Weaken – The Power Of NEXT
Jerry X Shea – 1st ed.

Includes bibliographical references.

ISNB 978-0-9712622-3-2

1. Inspirational 2. Self Help I. Shea, Jerry X   II. Title

Printed in the United States of America (USA) First Edition

This book is dedicated to my parents, Frank and Bettie Shea. Their love for each other gave me life and the ability to enjoy it. Their encouragement to always go for it and make it happen, *provided the inspiration necessary* for me to always take that next step.

WARNING-DISCLAIMER

Table of Contents

PART 11 - Page 137

NEXT – GO FOR IT AND MAKE IT HAPPEN

Introduction

How many times have you watched a television award show and the recipient gives a big *thank you* to someone for giving him the courage to *go for it.* Many times they thank God for their inspiration to move forward in life. Ever read an article about a successful person who, when asked *"To what do you attribute your success?"* answers, *"I just decided to go for it* and *make it happen."*

Go for it! Sounds simple enough, but what does it really mean? More importantly, how can you capture some of that *make it happen* attitude so that positive things can take place in your life? Answers to those questions, along with many life changing events, can be found in this book.

It is indeed a great life if we don't let life's happenings cause us to get weak. The power of this book, *It's A Great Life, If You Don't Weaken,* is limited only by your desire to find a better and more comfortable way to travel down that long and ever winding road we call life. This book can help you find some form of guidance, self-reassurance and a method of establishing a positive outlook. No one ever has a perfectly smooth ride. However, after you learn to commit yourself to a *go for it* attitude, the road will be less bumpy, seemingly dead ends will open up, and some of those rough turns will straighten out. As a result, you will find the way to *make it happen* and create positive experiences in your life.

I'm here to share with you a philosophy of life that I call *"next."* Through my principles of *next,* you too can experience the power of change, learning how to *go for it* and *make it happen. Next* will help you focus on the opportunities that come before you and provide the steps necessary for you to fulfill your dreams and goals. With my *next step* principles you will discover how to transform difficult situations into simple solutions. *Next* will help to keep you strong and not weak in life. *Next* will be there for you in those situations where you don't have the answer, can't find the solution, or can't think of what to do for right now. Learning to take that *next step* will help you move on to whatever you can do right now so that you will be able to continue with your life and not get stuck on hold.

Some chapters describe my life situations and experiences. Other chapters involve the lives of family and friends around me. A few true stories explore certain life happenings of people that have passed through my life and left a lasting impression on me. I would suggest first reading this book from cover to cover. Then, if necessary, go back and concentrate on the chapters that provide you with a challenge to make a real change in your life or that inspire you to focus your energy in a positive direction that, hopefully, will change your fate and destiny.

Through this book you will discover how using *next* in your life can help you obtain a happier family life, enjoy a healthier lifestyle, and experience less frustration, stress, and tension in your overall daily life. Learn what *next* is all about and how taking that *next step* can change your fate and destiny forever. While weak-minded people tend to fail in life, the strong seize those opportunities to *go for it* and *make it happen*. After all, when you stop and take a good look around you, I am sure you will agree that *It's A Great Life If You Don't Weaken.*

Jerry X Shea
Cambria, California

Part One

Understanding
NEXT

"Yesterday is history, tomorrow is a mystery, and today is a gift; that's why they call it the present."

Eleanor Roosevelt
(1884-1962)

Chapter 1

You Have Arrived

Relax. Take a deep breath, and clear your mind of all those activities that have taken place around you today. Now, ask yourself the following question: *"What life changing events have put me in the place that I am at right now in my life?"* I am not talking about the bookstore, supermarket, or the place you are with your e-book right now. That is just your physical location at this exact moment. The place I want you to focus on is the state and city where you reside, your workplace and the places you go to for fun and relaxation. Why, at this point in your life, are you physically going to those locations and not someplace else? What events in your life have put you *here* instead of *there*? More importantly, do you have a desire to be *there* instead of *here*?

In the same way that you have moved from one place to another in the physical sense, you have also moved around in an emotional and psychological sense. Your physical place in society, work, and home are really the end result of your emotional placement in life. Your actions or reactions, both physical and emotional, to the events and circumstances in your life were the motivational forces behind your physical location today.

In some cases there may have been events in your life in which you seemingly had no control. You may have been persuaded by others to go to a place where you really did not want to go to. You may even still be there.

I want you to relax and reach way back into the depths of your memory bank. Think back 5, 10 or 20 years ago. What was your life like at that time? Where did you live? What were you doing? Go ahead—take some more time and savor those thoughts.

Those images in your mind's eye that are popping up all around you of events from all those years gone by have created the person you are today. Whatever the events or circumstances may have been, they brought you to this very point in your life today. You can't change, alter, undo, make better, fix, or even relive any of those life experiences. The clock of life keeps ticking and you are moving right along with it. Everything that has happened to you makes you the person you are today. Your life's challenges, successes, failures and accomplishments have transformed you into the very person that others have come to know as *YOU.* Whoever *you* are and whatever *you* do, when *you* look in the mirror, there is no doubt that the image looking back, is, in fact, *you.*

So here *you* are and everyone knows you as *you.* Let me ask *you* the same question the caterpillar asked Alice in *Alice's Adventures In Wonderland*—*"Who are you?"* If I took five people who you feel know *you* really well, and asked them to describe *you,* would they all draw the same conclusion as to exactly who *you* are? Is there a chance that when they try to explain to me who *you* really are, as they feel they understand *you,* that will they be describing the outside *you* that *you* let them see? Could it be that there is another *you* on the inside that is just dying to break out, but can't? Are *you* so busy pleasing other people that *you* forgot to leave time for your own needs in life? Are you hiding a lifestyle that you think other people would not accept? Are you fearful of what might happen if *you* express your own needs? Is the real *you* someone who is suppressed by what others say? A person may go through his or her entire life with an inner voice begging to be set free. That person may possess a desire to be something other than the person many think they should be. Are *you* one of those people?

Did you ever read or hear about people who gave up six figure incomes to do missionary work or live in some small faraway village? Someone who stepped down from their climb up the corporate ladder to take a simple job that was less demanding or stressful. People have cashed in everything they owned to buy a boat and set sail for a trip around the world. Others have purchased a large motor home, pulled their kids out of schools, enrolled them in a correspondence course and, with the kids in tow, took off to see America.

There are many stories about people who suddenly change their course in life and move in a different direction. When that happens, everything that was in place falls out and their fates and destinies change forever.

Understanding Fate and Destiny

All the events that take place in your life going forward will continue to mold the person known as *you*. *You* have become the person *you* are because of how your fate and destiny have played out in your life to date. If you look in the dictionary for the definition of "fate," you will find that it states a word meaning "destiny." If you look up the word "destiny," you will find that one definition is "fate." Whereas fate and destiny have certain similarities and are sometimes used interchangeably, there are a few differences. Both words imply that all human activities are predetermined by a higher power. Most definitions of fate, however, go one step further to mean "the final outcome" or the "end," as in the statement: "it was fate that brought them together." In literature, fate sometimes emphasizes the irrationality and impersonal objective or cold nature of events, as in the statement: "The explorer's party left no trace of the fate that overcame them."

Destiny, on the other hand, is defined as "a culminating condition or an end which may be probable or inevitable." It means, in other words, the "continuing activity" or functional behavior that determines the eventual outcome. For example, "his destiny will be determined by his efforts today, to be the best in his field in the future."

Working within the definitions of fate as "an end result" and destiny as a "continuing activity," you can see that, as time goes on, the end result of the various events impacting your life will be your fate. The events that you are about to participate in *on a going forward basis*, on the other hand, will be your destiny. Keep in mind that once we play out the events in which we are to participate (our destiny), the end result becomes our fate.

Actually, your life in many respects is really fate, destiny, and then fate again. What you have done up to the present has been your fate, as many of these activities have reached their final outcomes, or end. Your continuing actions and behaviors going forward will determine your destiny. However, once you have reached the *culminating conditions* and achieve the final outcome or end, you will have met another fate for that point in time.

If you learn only one thing from this book, let it be an understanding that in one split second your fate or destiny can change forever. Something you do or even something you do not do could change your fate. An event or circumstance that happens around you or impacts you in any number of ways can change destiny. You may have your life all planned out when an accident happens, you are fired from your job, or you suddenly lose a loved one. When any of these events take place, everything changes. Just look at all the lives that changed forever when terrorists attacked the USA on September 11, 2001. When such an event occurs, like it or not, you will be forced to stop and reevaluate your life. After all, you had not planned on being fired, having an accident or losing a loved one. Should something come along that suddenly changes your fate or destiny, you will be forced to ask yourself, *"Now, what will be my next step?"*

Looking Back on Your Fate/Destiny

Take a moment now and imagine what your life would be like if you had turned one way instead of another at a major crossroad of your life? Maybe you thought you made the correct decision at the time, when, in fact, if you had taken another road, you could be in a much different place right now. But you are not someplace else, are you? Of course not. Thus, this is your fate right up to this point in your life. You cannot go back. So, going forward, what do you think you are destined to become or do in life?

The Time Frame of *"Next"*

What I want you to focus on now is that frame of time between your fate and your destiny. This is the point in time that I call *next*. It represents *the right now* when it comes to making a decision. *Next* is a life altering moment in which you choose to change your thought processes based on what is taking place right now in your life. From that moment forward, the decision you make at the moment of *next* gives you the ability to actually change your destiny, and thus, your fate. Changing how you think, what you do and how you go about doing it can result in a more exciting and fulfilling life. If your life turns out differently because of the changes you made, your fate and destiny will have also changed. The steps you take are what I call my *next step* principles for a better life going forward. What is really important for you to understand is that the decisions you make in your *next step* are not the same as mine. In fact, no two people have the same *next step* decisions to make.

When you *next* any of life's situations, you are actually determining what will take place *next* in your life. In that instant, you are determining the very next thing to do to gain control of your life or your situation. When you recognize the need for change in your life, you give yourself the greatest power of all. Allowing the person inside of *you* to step forward and show the world the real *you* is immensely rewarding .

When you think back on your life what do you think you could have done differently? What part of your education, or lack of it, would have changed your fate to date? Would you have married later, sooner or not at all? Would you have taken that job you were offered? Would you have moved to another state? If you could turn back the hands of time, knowing what you know today, what changes would you have made?

Is the reason you are not in a more comfortable position in life today the result of having accepted or settled for less yesterday? Are you just going through the motions of life because that is what your parents did? Or your brothers and sisters? Or your friends? Can you give me a good reason why you should not be in a better place in your life than you are right now? If you feel you are right where you want to be, just as you had planned it, and you have no desire to change anything, you are to be congratulated. You know who you are and where you are going in life. It should come as no surprise, however, that some people still have unfulfilled desires and don't know how to *go for it!* Still others can sense the need for change, but don't know what to do in order to *make it happen.*

Why do you have your current job? Maybe you took the job just to make some money or merely to have a job when you were younger. Why are you still working there? If you love your job, that is a different story. But chances are, you, like many other people, are not that satisfied with your job.

If you are unhappy with your place in life or the direction in which you are going, it is definitely time for you to take that *next step*. Your fate has put you where you are today. If, however, you have the courage within you to take control of your life and to make some changes, you can do something about the future. After all, this is your future we are talking about here. If you don't learn how to *next* your life situations and *go for it* and *make it happen*, your fate and destiny will not change. You will stay on the same path and will not see much positive change in your life going forward.

In many ways, without realizing it, you have already made changes in your fate and destiny. Stop for a moment and think of the times that you have had a desire to learn something new. Once you made the commitment, you moved forward with a great deal of excitement about it, right? You most likely had a desire to learn how to drive a car, even though it wasn't something that just came naturally to you. You were motivated by the thought of being able to drive yourself wherever you wanted to go and get your first taste of true independence. You did whatever you had to do to get that license. This, or course, including listening to your parents and putting up with whatever they said you had to do in order to pass that driver's test. When you stood in line at the department of motor vehicles, your fate stood in line with you. What would be your fate? Would you pass or would you fail? When you passed that driver's test, you met your fate. You were no longer destined to walk in order to get someplace. Did you change your fate and ultimately your destiny when it came to getting around? You bet you did!

When speaking to an audience, I can see that look of doubt on the faces of some of the attendees when I get to this part of the program. I know that look on their faces and I know what they are about to ask me. *"If someone learns to drive, gets in a car accident, and is killed or kills someone else, does that mean that it was that person's fate to die? After all, if the person never learned to drive, he would be alive or the other person they hit would not be dead."*

The answer to this is very simple. Our moment of death comes from a different point in time. It has nothing to do with the time on your wrist watch, but of a time in which clocks do not tick. Death is a certainty of life that we cannot control to a large extent. We have the power to prolong our life through healthy habits and the wisdom to know the consequences of taking physical risks. But normally, we do not control the moment of our death. This book is about the fate and destiny that you can control. It deals with your physical and emotional well-being. What happens to your body as the result of an accident and ultimately your death belongs to a much higher power. There are many books written on the subject of death and dying, but this book deals with the present and the joy of living.

What we need to do right now is to help you get into a frame of mind where you are able to give yourself permission to learn a new way of life, even if you have to work at it (like learning to drive) because it doesn't come naturally. To help you with that transition, I relate my story in the following chapter. I describe how I came to the realization of *next* and how powerful it could be in my life. After you understand how my philosophy of *next* became such an extraordinary part of my life, we will focus on helping you take that *next step* towards your life's desires, dreams and challenges. Once that is understood, we will concentrate on the *go for it* attitude. Finally, we will discuss the skills necessary to develop a *make it happen* attitude in your life.

Remember, what comes between fate and destiny is that short time frame of *next*. Change what you do *next* and you change your fate and destiny. Keep in mind that *it's a great life if you don't weaken.* So stay strong, give yourself permission to make some changes and then *go for it* and *make it happen.*

Chapter One Exercise

Here is a quick example of changing your fate and destiny. You get off work, get in your car, and head for home. If you go straight to your home— as you do every night— your fate and destiny will be a carbon copy of your drive home from the night before. Unless something at home has changed, you already know what your fate (when you get home) will be for the night. If, however, you are a man and you stop to purchase a dozen roses for your wife, or if you are a woman and you stop to buy your husband's his favorite ice cream for dessert, chances are your fate will change when you walk through that door. Your action may change your fate for the night. If you don't believe me, try it for yourself. The slightest change in your behavior has consequences.

In the simplest form, your fate may be only smelling the roses or eating the ice cream. Your destiny just might be in the hands of your spouse, but you will have at least made the gesture for a change in your destiny. What you have done is to *next* the moment with your action of buying roses or ice cream. So what will be your *next* move in life? Why not just *go for it* and see what happens?

For those of you who are single, you could also *next* the evening. Call a friend and suggest eating together tonight. Maybe you could barbecue, buy some take-out or try a new restaurant. Or, you could buy that ice cream, stop in after dinner to see a friend or relative you have not seen for a while and share the ice cream. The point here is to *next* the evening by doing something different. Now *go for it* and *make it happen.*

"I'm reminded of my parents' teachings… everything works out for the best and individuals determine their destiny through ambition and hard work."

Ronald W. Reagan
40th President of the United States
33rd Governor of California

Motivational speakers tend to stand at the bottom of the ladder trying to convince people what it is they need to do in order to climb up to the top.

Inspirational speakers, however, stand at the top, explain what it is they had to change in their life to get there, and then challenge others to find their own path up to the top.

Jerry X. Shea
Inspirational Speaker

Chapter 2

Setting The Stage

For NEXT

In order to get the full impact and understanding of how my philosophy of *next* can play such an important part in your life, you must first understand the basis of what makes *next* work, and where it came from.

Without even realizing it, the foundation for *next* was instilled into my way of thinking as I grew up. My parents raised my two younger sisters and me to develop minds of our own and not be persuaded by others. They taught us to look for the good and positive things in life and in people. But most important of all, they taught us not to labor over the process of making a decision. Whether we wanted to acquire a material object or just have fun doing something, if we had the financial means, felt the decision was morally correct, it would not harm anyone, and it was a goal we wanted to obtain or do, then my parents would encourage us to make the decision, feel good about that decision, and then *go for it*. My folks would always look at the options or benefits surrounding a change and then make a decision quickly. They did not labor over what to do. Once a decision was made, they would take the appropriate steps and then move on with their lives to whatever was *next*.

While celebrating New Year's Eve in 1952, my folks started talking about leaving Massachusetts and moving to California. They weighed benefits, looked at their options and decided to *go for it*. They put their house up for sale in January of 1953. Within six months from their first discussions of making the move, our family was in Los Angeles. They made it happen.

When I became a teenager, it was apparent that not all families lived the same kind of lives or had the same kind of values that my parents had. Our parents let us make decisions on things that related just to us. I can remember my mother always saying *"Just make up your mind as to what you want to do and then do it."*

In high school there were six of us that hung around together and when we graduated in 1961, all six of us answered the call of President John F. Kennedy and joined the service. We wanted to do our part to protect the USA from communism. I went into the U.S. Navy and I don't think I did too much to fight communism while stationed in Meridian, Mississippi and then San Diego, California, but I did take the opportunity to extend my love of photography and became a Navy photographer.

If there was ever a point in my life in which I felt that I had grown up fast, it had to be my four years away from home in the Navy. It was at this point that I came face-to-face with some of my first challenges in life. Suddenly I found myself in an arena with so many different personalities. I tried hard to understand why some people had thoughts and perceptions of other people that were so different from my own. I witnessed prejudices (especially in Mississippi) like I had never seen growing up, or had ever been exposed to previously! I quickly understood that while there was an assortment of different values for many people, some had no value system at all. I met people who only cared about themselves and worst of all, would do anything to anyone if they could benefit from it. At the same time, I met people who thought the way I did and seemed to have a sense of values and ethics in their lives that matched mine. They were the ones I would gravitate towards and I surrounded myself with their friendship.

One very interesting observation I had about the service was how so many people with complex personalities and differences could come together as a whole when working towards a defined goal, and how hard everyone was willing to work at the task of achieving that goal. This made it a *next* for everyone! Irrespective of what the person's thoughts may have been on religion, politics, raising children, or the opposite sex, everyone worked together as a team. Once the task was completed or the goal met, it was amazing to me how each person would switch back to their beliefs, value systems and prejudices and continue on in their own way.

Then there were the lost souls. These people had absolutely no direction in their lives whatsoever. They had no idea what they wanted to do in life, or what their purpose in life should be. The sad part for young people like this is that they were the perfect prey for people who were strong-minded and manipulative. These people were looking for young minds to recruit and bring into their political cause, protest, or religious movement. Worst of all, these stronger minded people could usually persuade these lost souls to hate others or take part in acts of violence. The April 19, 1995, Oklahoma bombing by Timothy McVeigh and Terry Nichols is a perfect example of such thinking.

My experience in the Navy was another step for me in setting my standards for *next* as a way of life. I refused to get upset over any situation that I could not change. It made more sense to me to just say *"next,"* do what had to be done, and move on with my life. To spend half of the day griping about what had to be done was a waste of my time and energy. I decided that *next* would become my motto for accepting the things that I could not change and motivating myself towards the things I had to do and could change.

The greatest impact on my way of thinking and validation for my belief that *next* would be my way of life, came in 1965 after I got out of the Navy and went to work at Saint John's Hospital and Health Center in Santa Monica, California. I was hired as the first Biomedical Photographer in the hospital's newly formed cardiovascular department. My experience and knowledge with high speed motion picture cameras, film processing equipment and other specialized photographic systems, all of which I learned in the Navy, gave me an advantage over other applicants for the position.

Saint John's Hospital, along with UCLA Medical Center and the Veterans Administration Hospital in Los Angeles, were each involved in a program with doctors from all three hospitals perfecting and performing open heart surgeries. They had progressed from surgery on animals at UCLA (yes, contrary to what you may have heard about animal rights, at UCLA they performed open heart surgery on large animals to make sure the heart-lung machine could keep them alive) to saving the lives of humans. Because open heart surgery was in its early pioneering stages, there was a real need to document everything about each patient in order to help diagnose heart disease and prevent heart attacks in others. My initial job was to document, through 16mm movies (they did not have video back then) and still photographs, the different operating procedures, techniques, and pathological findings on patients undergoing open heart surgery. I would put together films for doctors to show to their peers at medical seminars, and less bloody films to show to the public about the advances in open heart surgery. For twelve years my photographs (still and motion) documented the heart disease problems and conditions of the patients. When a patient died and the doctors performed an autopsy, I would take pictures of the heart to document clogged coronary arteries and other defects of the heart.

I eventually became a cardiac technician and part of the open heart surgery team. We worked with and witnessed the evolution of the heart-lung machine from a very complicated fixed oxygenator (the part of the machine that puts oxygen into the patient's blood) to the disposable oxygenator that reduced the tear down, reassemble and sterilization time from over twelve hours to less than 30 minutes. The disposable oxygenator took us from two surgeries a week to two surgeries a day, if needed.

A diagnostic procedure that the doctors used to help diagnose heart disease was a test called a cine-angiogram that was performed during a heart catheterization. The special equipment utilized a 35mm high speed camera that took moving X-ray pictures of the heart as it functioned. With the aid of a special dye injected through a catheter the films highlighted the coronary arteries (the arteries that feed the heart muscle itself), the valves of the heart, and the chambers of the heart. The same test was also performed on the carotid arteries that supply blood to the brain. Shot at high speed, the films were reviewed in slow motion. The purpose of the test was to locate narrowing of the coronary or carotid arteries caused by arteriosclerosis or atherosclerosis. Arteriosclerosis is the thickening and hardening of the walls of the arteries. Atherosclerosis is the deposit of fatty material in the arteries, referred to as plaque, which in time narrows or completely blocks off the flow of blood through the arteries. If there is complete blockage (occlusion) of a coronary artery, the flow of blood carrying oxygen needed to feed the heart muscle (called the myocardium) via that coronary artery will be stopped and the tissue in that section of the heart muscle will die. If a large section of the muscle dies off, the heart will have a hard time trying to pump blood. Whether the patient will recover or pass through that tunnel of white light to the great beyond depends on how many arteries are blocked, or how much of the myocardium dies off. Blockage in the carotid arteries and lack of oxygen to the brain will result in a stroke or even death.

Through my job, I had the opportunity to look at every patient's chart that passed through that cardiovascular department in a twelve year period. Imagine being twenty or thirty years old and having the opportunity to read every chart of patients' who had a heart attack or stroke. Believe me, it would change your way of thinking about your health as it did for me. When I came to the section entitled Physical and History (on the patient chart), I noticed that each patient's report read almost like a copy of every other patient ahead of them. This is because many of these patients undergoing the angiogram or having open heart surgery (with the exception of those born with a heart problem) all lived the same kind of lifestyle. They smoked cigarettes (and if you saw what happens, not only to your heart but also to your lungs, you would never touch a cigarette), and they ate a lot of meat and other fatty foods, including bacon and eggs every day. They consumed lots of dairy products and deep fried foods. They drank too much alcohol and worked in high stress jobs. But the one element that was really bringing them onto that operating table and into surgery was the fact that for most of them, the last time they vigorously exercised was in high school or college.

One of the most shocking medical reports that the doctors would use in their talks while showing films and photographs that I took for them, was an article first published in the Journal of the American Medical Association (JAMA) on July 18, 1953 titled "Coronary Disease Among United States Soldiers Killed in Action in Korea." The article stated "that of the autopsies performed on 300 soldiers killed in action between the ages of 18 and 48, with the average age being 22.1 years, 77.3% of their hearts had some gross evidence of coronary atherosclerosis. The disease process varied from *"fibrous thickening to large athermanous plaques causing complete occlusion of one or more of the major vessels (coronary)."*

While researching this book, I came across a reprint of that original article in a JAMA reprint dated November 28, 1985, and this time it stated that *"the article (original) appeared at a time when mortality from coronary heart disease was reaching a zenith in the United States and being recognized worldwide as a modern epidemic."* (see page 35).

In July 2000, the American Heart Association's issue of Circulation had a report from researchers led by Dr. Henry C. McGill Jr. of the Southwest Foundation for Biomedical Research in San Antonio, Texas. It read, in part, *"... pored over the autopsies of 760 young men and woman who died in accidents, homicides or suicides. Arterial blockage was found in 2 percent of the 15- to 19-year old boys who were studied, and in about 20 percent of the men ages 20-34. Even though a small number of the teen-agers had clogged arteries, researchers were surprised to see any at all."* (Read that again and you can understand why doctors are so concerned with the obesity problem in young children.)

It is very important to note that for many years leading up to the fifties, a heart attack for a man under 60 years of age was considered an executive disease. That's because these persons entered into and enjoyed a leisurely lifestyle. Unfortunately, they stopped physical exercise. As vigorous exercise decreased and the availability of fatty foods increased, the ages of men having heart attacks started to drop into the 50s, and 40s age group. Throw in some daily stress and you have people in their 30s having heart attacks. Enter the women's liberation movement of the '60s and suddenly you have more women going into the workplace taking on those high stress jobs. Many do not have an exercise program, eat the wrong foods, drink more, smoke, and are experiencing high stress.. The end result, more females with heart problems.

Now here is the kicker. Although the different procedures during open heart surgery may have saved a person's life, doctors were still faced with a concern. Here we had a patient whose life was saved through the wonders of modern medicine, but the patient's life was really stuck on hold. Yes, the doctors saved their life, but what kind of life did the person come from and what kind of a life would he or she go back to? Obviously, if the patient continued to live the life that brought him to the open heart surgery table in the first place, he would undoubtedly end up right back in the hospital again, if he didn't die first.

Prior to the advances of open heart surgery, a patient who suffered a heart attack became a heart cripple. Many were bedridden, afraid to move fast and didn't exercise. All activities, including going back to work had to be rest related. In short, the patient may have survived the heart attack, but he became a "heart cripple" to the excitement of life because of the fear of having another heart attack.

Then came cardiac rehabilitation. The solution to helping the patient after open heart surgery or the patient that had survived a heart attack. Instead of keeping the patient in bed for weeks after open heart surgery, the doctors had them up, out of bed, and on their feet within two or three days. Before the end of a week, they were walking the halls. Within a month they were on exercise bikes in the Cardiac -

Rehabilitation Department. Dietitians explained to them and their families the correct diets and how to shop for healthy foods. The transformation from the out of shape, overweight patients that were not living healthy life-styles to the trimmed down, into exercise healthy person took place in just six to eight weeks. Many would say "I haven't felt this great since I was in high school." Even patients that had suffered an actual heart attack and went through cardiac rehabilitation became healthier patients.

There is no doubt that cardiac rehabilitation was the ultimate *next step* for these patients and did indeed change their fate and destiny.

With twelve years in that cardio-vascular department, I witnessed thousands of open heart surgeries, heart catheterizations, and patients with heart related problems. That experience gave me the opportunity to see firsthand how eating unhealthy foods, smoking, stress and most important of all, a sedentary lifestyle, can indeed shorten someone's life.

All of these hard facts continued to underscore my concept of *next* and how it could indeed change a person's fate and destiny. The most significant fact of all was the realization of how important a part exercise, combined with the correct diet, could play in the quality of one's life. Now, some forty years after I first went to work in that cardiovascular department, it has been pretty well documented that if you smoke, overindulge in fatty foods, don't exercise, gain excessive weight and live a stressful lifestyle like those patients did, you, too, could end up a good candidate for open heart surgery, if you don't die first.

But wait until you read this. In 2006 the American Heart Association reported that *for the first time ever, more woman between 55 and 65 died of cardiovascular disease than men.* Women who stayed at home involved in *housework*, didn't realize it but all that washing, ironing, scrubbing and keeping up a house was exercise. Now, for many women in the workplace, they have no exercise program. Just like men, they come home tired from the day and just want to relax. The end result, women are now dying ahead of men. While those in the women's movement of the '60s wanted to prove they could succeed *in a man's world* and even *do a better job*, I don't think the woman's movement ever set a goal to *beat out men in death*, yet it is indeed one of the end results of women in the workplace. (See the stats on page 34.)

Today, with the knowledge of how important exercise can be to extending your life, and how building up your muscles can not only help strengthen your legs and arms, but enhance your overall exercise program, people everywhere are joining health clubs in cities throughout the country.

Now that you have an overview of how important health is in understanding *next*, let's stop right here and talk about *you*. How is the old body anyway? Are you the correct weight for your height? Do you treat your body the way you want your children or grandchildren to treat their bodies? No one expects you to be in line for the next cover of Vogue or GQ. However, if you're a man, does your stomach stick out like you're the first male about to give birth? Are you a woman that looks pregnant, but you're not? Would you be a good candidate for the before shot in some health magazine? Granted, some people have come into this world with a built-in weight problem. But just because you're at the top of weight, height, and bone structure statistics is no excuse for putting on weight that is above and beyond what your body needs.

And what do you put into your body anyway? Are you working hard at developing cancer by smoking? Can you go a week without taking one alcoholic drink? Do you take pills, drugs and who knows what else to get through the day? Do you really care about your body? Maybe you think your body will just take care of itself. If you do think that, then it is time to change your thinking. After all, you would have to be oblivious to every medium around you to not know all the statistics that have been brought out about smoking, drinking, weight control, exercise, healthy foods and just plain health in general. That light bulb in your brain is definitely not too bright if you continue to do unhealthy things to your body. And you're making a very important mistake if you don't take the time to look into the facts of a healthier lifestyle.

Did you know that up until the '80s, many fast food restaurants cooked their french fries in lard? Just in case you're young enough to have never heard of lard, lard is nothing more than pork fat, 100% pure pork fat. It was (and still is in some places) used for deep frying foods. People started making noise about restaurants using lard and many changed to low cholesterol, low fat cooking oils. Today, I don't think a restaurant or fast food chain could stay in business if it used lard in their cooking. Unfortunately, however, there are still many small food stands and even independent restaurants that still use lard and you should keep away from them.

While the drive to stop the use of lard was big in the '80s, the big push in the mid-2000s was to eliminate trans fats completely in restaurants. Overall changes like these are designed to aid in a positive diet for the American public, especially when you consider the fact that a large number of people, left to their own devices, can't seem to make positive health changes on their own.

Irrespective of your age, if by now you are not aware of the right foods to eat and how exercise plays an important part in your well-being, then you too, will be a candidate for a heart attack or stroke. You may even need open heart surgery one day. That is, of course, if the heart attack doesn't just up and kill you before the doctors can perform the surgery. The people who are aware of and follow how much a correct diet and a good exercise program play in their everyday health and longevity will be reading about you in the local obituary column. Face it, your health is a key factor in your ability to enjoy your everyday life. Your health is a gift. Health is also a key elements in making *next* and *next step* work for you.

Do you think you will make it to age 80 and still be active if you keep living your life the way you have been living it? Remember, your fate and destiny is under *your* control. If you are destined to have a heart attack because you don't live a healthy lifestyle, then take that *next step* and change your health habits today. In fact, why not *go for it* right now and *make it happen?*

From the American Heart Association

To get the latest statistics on heart disease go to the American Heart Association (AMA) website at www.heart.org. While researching for this book, I about fell off of my chair when I saw that in 2006, *for the first time ever*, more woman between the ages of 55-64 died of cardiovascular disease (CVD) than men: 52.9% male deaths, 56.5 % female deaths. Total CVD deaths (all ages) in 2006 = 831,272.

Of all the deaths

- Nearly 37% were current smokers (in last 12 months)
- More than 75% were overweight and 45% were obese.
- 45% participated in no physical activity

Other causes of death in 2006:

Cancer............559,888

Accidents..........121,599

HIV (AIDS)....... 12,113

One in two women will eventually die of heart disease or stroke; one in twenty-five women will eventually die of breast cancer.

What is an MI

Myocardial infarction or MI is caused when the coronary arteries build up with plaque, and block off or stop the flow of blood to the myocardium (the heart muscle) which causes that part of your heart muscle to die. If too much of the heart muscle dies, you get "sudden cardiac death," of which 90% of the cases are due to coronary heart disease. Sometimes, unfortunately, the first symptom of heart disease is indeed *sudden death*.

In the 1985 reprint of the JAMA article, the last paragraph was titled "Significance of this Report" and reads as follows;

"The significance of this 1953 LANDMARK ARTICLE for physicians, health educators, and the public today is that the answer to CHD (coronary heart disease) is prevention and that preventive measures for this most important disease process must begin early in life. This observation does not mean that preventive measures designed to retard the progression of atherosclerosis should not be used in middle-aged and older individuals, but only that for maximum benefit, preventive efforts should be directed toward the young."

Here are 13 unlucky famous people who dropped dead of a heart attack or stroke under the age of 60.

Name	Occupation	Age of death
1. John Candy	Comic/Actor	43
2. Ian Fleming	Author, James Bond novels	56
3. Jim Fixx	Author & long distance runner	52
4. Jerry Garcia	Lead guitar -Grateful Dead	53
5. Clark Gable	Actor	59
6. Roy Orbison	Singer (Pretty Woman)	52
7. Robert Palmer	British Rock Star	54
8. Rod Serling	Writer/Director – The Twilight Zone (smoked 4 packs a day)	51
9. Tim Russet	Moderator of Meet the Press	59
10. Phil Harris	Fisherman/Captain, Deadliest Catch	53
11. Luther Vandross	Singer	54
12. Robert Shaw	Actor, Jaws, The Sting	51
13. Andrew Breitbart	Commentator/blogger	43

The list of early deaths due to heart attacks (and many brought on by smoking), are but a few of the people who lost their lives much too soon in life. When you look at any list of people that died early because of lung cancer, again brought on by smoking, you really do have to re-evaluate your lifestyle if you smoke, eat unhealthy food, gain weight, don't exercise and have stress in your life.

Yes, we are all going to die one day. The question is, "will it be sooner or later?" No one in their right mind would want to die sooner. Now _go for it_ and live a long life.

"Sometimes the shortest distance between here and success turns out to be the long way around."

Jerry X Shea

Chapter 3

The Long Climb Up To
The NEXT STEP

A major driving force in working with *next* comes from having been in a *good spot* in life and then suddenly tumbling down. You may have read various business success stories in which someone that was *on top* suddenly took *a fall*. Through hard work, diligence, a positive attitude, and applying *next* to the situation, that person made it back on top. This is because they have previously been in a successful place. They know what it was like to be a major player in life's happenings. For that reason, they often have a positive outlook, work harder, longer, and draw on all of their life's experiences to make it back to the top after they fall.

Like many other people, I too have gone from the *mountain of success* to the *valley of lost dreams*. It is in that valley, with only one direction to go, that I took a deep breath and started the long and courageous struggle back up the mountain. Stumbling, falling, getting knocked down, I kept on trying to inch my way back to the top.

Nothing exemplifies using *next* better than my seven-year climb out of that *valley* after I had to close my business. I worked harder than I ever had before to get back to the top again.

Here is my full story. As I related in chapter two, I was in my 20s when I started working at Saint John's Hospital and Health Center in Santa Monica, California. That was my Monday through Friday job. Being young and eager to get ahead in life, I also had two weekend jobs. One was as a wedding and baby photographer, which proved to be very lucrative. The other money making and fun job was that of a bartender for private parties. Living near Beverly Hills, Malibu, and other affluent communities, a weekend never went by that someone wasn't having a private party and needed bartenders. I even bartended the PGA Golf Tournament in Brentwood, California four years in a row. This extra work helped build up a solid savings that brought in enough cash that on my 25th birthday I was able to buy the car of my dreams a Jaguar XKE. For my 28th birthday I purchased my first home while I was still single (have owned five to date). Eventually, I dropped the wedding, baby pictures, and bartending jobs and started making 16mm sound films for the medical community. As a freelance film producer, I found my vacations turning into location shoots. I even ended up in Ethiopia, Africa, shooting a film on the Omo River.

At age 31, I married the greatest woman in the world, my loving wife Mary (see Chapter 19), and by age 33 purchased a house with an indoor swimming pool and an unobstructed view of the city. There was no doubt that we were living the good life. My 16mm film production business was getting to a point of becoming a full time job. After 12 years with the cardiovascular department and 4 years with the Department of Education at the hospital, I quit my job and went full time with my production company.

Life seemed great in my 20s and 30s. The finer things in life that I had come to enjoy and worked so hard to maintain, came to an end, however, when I turned 42 years old.

Without going into great detail, the lower cost of video production compared to the expense of 16mm sound films forced me and many other small film production companies right out of business.

It was bad enough that I was faced with the challenge of "now what do I do?," but my wife suddenly found her employer, Western Airlines *("the only way to fly")* about to file bankruptcy and she would be out of a job. We realized that making mortgage payments on a home that required two incomes was not going to cut it if we were both out of work. We eventually sold our home, paid off all our debts, cut back on expenses and rented a condominium. You can believe me when I say that celebrating my 42nd birthday in a rented condo was not the image I had in mind at that point in my life.

On top of that our kids just didn't know what to make of the sudden changes. After all, they were the kids that had been living in the house with the indoor pool and now they lived in a condo on a busy street. If there was ever a time in my life that I wish I could have changed the way things were, it was then, or so it seemed at that time.

When someone loses a job, as bad as it may seem at first, most people feel that they can take what they have learned on that job and offer their knowledge to a new employer. This is called *employability* or *marketability.* This is one reason why everyone should learn as much as they can in any job. It is a different story, however, when a person owns a company that provided a product/service that no one wants or needs any more. It is quite a shock to wake up one morning and realize that you not only don't have a business anymore, you don't have a job or a place to go for work. To make matters even worse, you are no longer *marketable* because the market for your service/product has disappeared.

My wife moved on to other employment and became the bread winner in the family. In order to bring in some form of income, I took a sales job selling yellow page advertising and was the oldest person in the sales group of 24 on our team. Surrounded by college graduates with no family responsibilities and trying to get back on my feet financially, I couldn't even afford to join them for lunch at a restaurant and instead took a brown bag lunch to work each day.

It was about two months after I took the job selling yellow page advertising that I pulled my van into a convenience store to get a drink to go with my brown bag lunch. I walked out with my drink, got into my van, went to take a bite of my sandwich, and just broke down into tears. I cried and cried and cried, almost to the point of hysteria. I couldn't stop crying. I had remained strong and kept a positive attitude for the last year and a half as I closed down my business and sold off all of the company's assets. Now I had a job that I hated. The emotions finally caught up with me. No matter how you cut it, I no longer had a business and was no longer working in the field that I took an interest in at the age of 12. My world as I knew it had come crashing down around me.

I managed to pull myself together, looked around expecting to see people pointing at the grown man crying. Of course I was relieved to find that no one saw me, however, my shirt and tie where soaking wet. I got out of the van and took a walk around the block to try and dry out. I reminded myself of how I could not change fate, but I could sure change my destiny. It was time for me to *next* the negative situations around me and take that ever important *next step* necessary to make changes in my life going forward.

When I got back to the van, I took out a sheet of paper and drew a line down the middle. On the left side I wrote the positive highlights of my life up to that point in time. On the right I listed the negative thoughts that where pulling me down. When I looked at what I had written, I realized that I had accomplished a lot of things in life that other people only dreamed of doing. I had worked hard all my life and that hard work had paid off. I was married to a wonderful woman that never came down on me for the loss of my business. The kids, my wife and I were all healthy. We also had a roof over our heads, which was more than what some people had. The bottom line became apparent. I was not going to hell in a hand basket and life was indeed great.

I took a few deep breaths and said to myself, "*the past is past --- it was my fate --- it's over --- NEXT. Now what are you going to do with the rest of your life Shea?*" With that thought, I started to write down a set of goals for my life going forward.

I have always been a goal setter and I knew the difference between realistic and unrealistic goals. It would have been unrealistic to set any type of goal that would have transformed me from this down and out point in my life right back on top in a heartbeat. However, as a long range goal, without a time frame on it, I set a goal of someday owning my own business again. The key word here is *someday.* I did not say in one year or five years, just *someday.* For now, that was enough of an overall long range goal to kick start positive thinking. The hard part was, what did I have to do in order to reach that goal?

First of all, I knew it would take money to get back in business and for working capital. Had this happened to me when I was young, money would not have been an issue because there would have been only me. But now I was married and had financial responsibilities far beyond just myself. Knowing that it will take money to own a business, I had to figure out what I had to do in order to get that money and still contribute to the household.

I had to decide just what I wanted to do for the rest of my life. What would I need to do in order to lift myself up financially? More importantly, what did I like to do? I thought about that for a while. Then I started writing down the things I did and didn't like to do. One thing I knew that I did not want to do was work back in film production. I had *been there, done that.* I wanted to move on in life. But what did I enjoy doing? What was it that I enjoyed during all those years of film production, working at the hospital, photographing weddings and baby pictures, being a bartender? It was people. That was it! *I enjoyed working and dealing with people.*

Did this mean I should focus on become a social worker? Go back into the hospital arena? I don't think so. Yes, I enjoyed people, and I spent 12 out of 16 years at the hospital helping heart patients. I wanted to move away from that area also. People? What could I do that would keep me in front of people while at the same time make the kind of money I needed to get ahead so that I could, once again, own my own business and be my own boss?

Then it hit me. What did I enjoy doing 20 years ago when I talked to a couple that was getting married and looking for a wedding photographer? What gave me that great feeling when I talked to parents about shooting pictures of their baby? What was that high I got when leaving the offices of the big executives that had just hired me to shoot the 16mm films for their company? *YES! THAT WAS IT!* I enjoyed the *"SALE."*

YES, sales. I always enjoyed the fact that I was able to convince the young couple to hire me to shoot their wedding pictures. I sold my talent and persuaded the parents to hire me to take pictures of their children. I presented my abilities to the executives and gave them a good reason to hire my company to create their promotional film. That was it all right, I enjoyed *selling.* It put me in front of people who wanted to buy something that I had to offer. If I did my job right, they would buy from me. If they bought from me, I would make money. Suddenly I had a focus for what type of job I wanted to do going forward in life? *Sales* it would be.

Although I had a job selling yellow page advertising, I was looking at it as *just a job* until I got my feet on the ground and figured out what to do with the rest of my life. The problem with having *just a job* is the old acronym for *J-O-B* = *Just Over Broke.* This of course was reflected in the low commissions I was receiving with my *just a job* attitude. On top of that I viewed being the oldest person in my group as a down fall in my life. My weakness could be found in the fact that I had lost my focus on just *who was I.* Obviously my life's lessons and abilities surpassed those other team members half my age. Now, all of that was about to change. I set a short term goal right then and there. First, I would work as hard as I could. Second, focus on being the top sales person. Third, as much as I thought that I hated my job, I would turn that hate around and into a *next* with a *go for it* and *make it happen* attitude. After all, I had two choices that were clearly mine and mine alone. I could continue to hate my job and let it pull me down even lower. Or, I could turn that hate into productive energy and eventually more money.

Realizing I had hit the bottom when I broke down and cried, I now had to work on getting back on top. It was time to change the direction of my destiny by taking it off of *hold* and moving forward in life. I knew I would have to work for other people and take on tasks that I would not enjoy, but, I could finally see a tiny little light at the end of that long dark tunnel. My goal was to get to the end of it and step out into the light. I was ready for that *next step* to change my fate and destiny. It was time to *go for it* and I was definitely going to *make it happen.*

Two months later I was indeed the top sales person on our team and stayed that way all the time I worked for the company. One of the first highlights of turning my life around came when some of the *young kids* started asking me for advice. They wanted to know what they could do to *make it happen* in their sales efforts. Without even setting it as a goal, I became a mentor to some of those younger salespeople.

What took place over the following seven years could be a book in and of itself. It was the result of working hard, keeping my eyes and ears open to everything around me as I listened to the life and working experiences of other people. Most important of all, I worked very hard at *making it happen* for me and for those around me by doing the best I could at whatever job I was doing.

Every job I took was a commissioned sales job. If I could not make the sale, there would be no money. It was that simple. I had many different sales jobs in a 7 year period. The longest held job at one place was 2 1/2 years. The shortest was 2 1/2 hours when the owner lied to three of us and we all walked out the door.

My father had spent his whole life as a car salesmen so I gave it a try selling Hondas and later Volvo's. At the end of the 80's I sold Jaguar automobiles and then the Lexus when it first came out. I ended up getting a real estate license in 1990 and went to work for a business broker helping people buy or sell business opportunities.

One month before my 49th birthday and seven years after I sat in that parking lot crying, I walked out of the proverbial long dark tunnel and into the sunlight on January 15, 1992. That was the day I reached my long range goal and purchased a six year old screen printing company that produced T-shirts for the local community. Once again, I owned my own business and became my own boss. What took place in my life for that seven year period was worth more than money could buy. As hard as those days may have been (especially after closing my business), they actually gave me the opportunity to grow and learn more about myself, life, people, and business experiences than I could have ever learned from the finest business school in the country. My education was an actual life and business experience. Napoleon Hill in his book Think and Grow Rich refers to my form of education as a degree from the *University of Hard Knocks, UHK*. What I learned and how I progressed in those years can never be taken away from me. As it turns out, they represent some of the best years of my life as they pertain to personal growth. They were not the worst years of my life as it seemed at that time. I implemented that knowledge into my new business, making sure that the mistakes witnessed at other businesses, especially the ones I saw when I sold business opportunities, were not brought into my business. As the owner, I was responsible for payroll, banking, expenses and all the other business concerns that go with owning one's own business. While the employees did the work of screen printing the images on the T-shirts, my part in this business during the 9 to 5 hours of operation was to do what I realized I do best, *sales*. My job, in order to keep the company going strong, was to focus on selling the capabilities of my company, Icon Imprinted Sportswear.

What was a small screen printing company when I purchased it became one of the largest screen printing and embroidery companies in Torrance, California. After eight years of ownership I sold the business in 1999. My wife and I retired out of the Los Angeles area to Cambria, California.

I decided to put my business brokering and the success of my company into book form and in 2001 self-published my first book *IT LOOKS EASY! IS IT? Simple Steps For*

Small Business Success. I designed some small business workshops, based on my book, and put the wheels in motion for a speaking career. While I knew that would take time to develop and since 15 months had passed since we left LA, my wife and I both had a burning desire to *have something to do* right now. So we both went to work for a local real estate company.

Day one at that real estate office was another life changing event for both of us. We went to work for an independent real estate office called Pines By The Sea Properties. The office had nine other agents that had roots in the community, while we had none. This small town of Cambria also had 106 other realtors working in one of 22 real estate offices. On top of that a total of only 45 homes where for sale. There was no doubt that we were starting our new real estate careers at the very bottom. Using what I had outlined in my book *IT LOOKS EASY! IS IT? Simple Steps for Small Business Success* and from a dead start in January 2002 we finished our first year in real estate by coming in third in overall sales for the agency.

Then a few months later the owner of one of the local coffee/espresso shops in town (this small town had 6 of them) asked us to represent him in the sale of his business. After Mary and I reviewed his financials and talked with him about his business, we decided to buy The Cambria Coffee Den Roasting Company. Then to our surprise, a few months after our purchase of the coffee shop the owners of Pines by the Sea Properties decided to sell their home and move back east. Having spent over a year and a half under the umbrella of that real estate company we struck a deal with the outgoing owners and purchased the goodwill of Pines by the Sea Properties, the very real estate company we had gone to work for almost two years earlier. We opened our real estate office in the same building as the coffee shop and relished the opportunity of running our businesses and becoming a part of the community. I even started a Toastmasters club in Cambria.

While we ran those businesses I also started building my speaking career. I developed small business workshops on how to prospect for new clients, how to give a presentation that makes the prospect say *"I want to go with your company"* and how to close the sale. I became a key note speaker for business groups and conducted my classes at small business expos. I spoke at chambers of commerce luncheons and wrote small business articles for magazines. In February of 2011, I came out with my second small business book, *Prospecting – Presentation – Close, Your Three Keys To Successful Sales.*

When we would tell people what we did, many thought we were working ourselves to death. The truth is we were having a fun time doing what we do in our so called retirement from the big city. We knew how to find the right balance between work, family, social and private life. We made sure that when we take that *next step* we have thought it out, planned it out and made adjustments so it fits into what we want in life. We made time for morning exercise and quiet time together. Everything else is just *going for it* and *making it happen* as we travel down our roads of life.

In fact, traveling down that road has also changed. As of 2007, we sold our coffee shop and traveled to my speaking engagements in a 40-foot motor home coach over a four month period. We had so much fun that in 2008 we took a nine month trip while I spoke. The beauty of this form of travel is that we take our time getting to the speaking engagement as we see America. Realizing we had discovered a whole new lifestyle that we both loved, we eventually closed our real estate office, rented out our house and moved into our motor home full time. We had reached another one of life's Milestones - no responsibilities to anyone (employees) but to ourselves and no reason to have to stay put in one place. This is a very fun time in our lives as we leave our late 60s and look forward to what the new decade has to offer. So much fun, that by the time this book is published, we will be going into our fourth year of living full time in our motor home. By the end of 2013 we will have visited all 49 states, from Fairbanks, Alaska to Key West, Florida and San Diego, California to Bar Harbor, Maine, and every state in-between. Our address ---- *someplace in the U.S.A.*

Many folks look down life's roads and see *do not enter.* When we look, we see *open roads ahead.* What do you see?

Note: For the record, we use a mail forwarding service to get our mail, but receive very little. Most of our needs are conducted via the Internet.

Chapter Assignment

Draw a line down the center of a piece of paper and on the left side list all the positive things in your life. Write as many as you can. On the right hand side list the negative things in your life. Now look at what you have written very carefully. Did you write down the truth, or hold something back? No one else is going to look at this (unless you show them) so be honest with yourself and list as many positive and negative things about your life as you can think of.

Now look at what you have before you. Study both sides carefully. You are looking at the *ups* and *downs* in your life at this very moment in time.

Go back to the bottom of page 42 and re-read what I did when I listed the positive and negative things in my life. Now start working on changing your negatives to positives and along the way you'll find your destiny will be changed. *Go for it* and *make it happen. Next.*

Even if you're on the right track,
you'll get run over if you just sit there.

Will Rogers

Stress is created by a person's attitude towards life in general and their job in particular.

Jerry X. Shea

Chapter 4

NEXT–

Do You Have Stress in Your Life?

Having reviewed the effects of certain foods and lack of exercise on the physical body in Chapter Two, you will also need to understand how the body reacts to stress, anxiety, and frustration in order to gain control of your fate and destiny, and to get *next* to work for you.

When you learn to recognize all the negative forces and elements that surround you on a daily basis, and how they cause you to get up tight and tense, then you will have taken the *next step* in reducing your stress. The desire to get that stress out of your life will also require a deeper understanding of how your body and mind work together.

As with most things in life, there are usually two (or more) viewpoints. When it comes to personalities in general, you will find them broken down into two types. Type A and type B. The Type A personality is usually perceived as being very active, usually talks fast, moves fast, and takes command of situations. A Type A person will let it all out when they are upset. As a result, people think that Type As never get ulcers or become stressed out because they let off steam and get things off their chests.

In contrast, Type B people are typically quiet and reserved. They do not jump into conversations quickly. They move slower and let others take control without voicing their opinions. These people usually keeps their thoughts and feelings to themselves. People tend to think that the Type B person is not really bothered by any particular situation.

The problem is that both Type A and Type B persons can become *stressed-out*. They can both become candidates for a heart attack or stroke. Even though Type A people appear as if they are *getting it off of their chests*, they often do not really know how to let it go. They may still keep the problem that is bothering them inside, let it boil, and not know how to *next* the situation. Type B persons, although they do not verbalize how they feel, will also let the situation eat them up inside. They, too, may not know how to use *next*.

Let's talk about stress in the workplace for a moment. Just reading or hearing that very sentence could cause your blood pressure to rise. Right? Well, let's look at what gives you stress at work. First, believe it or not, the company is not the cause of your stress. Now, before you say, *"Oh yes it is,"* just hear me out and think about it for a minute. If you feel you have a stressful job, you need to take a good look at what you do. Try breaking it down and finding out just what it is that creates this stress. The company and place you work are not necessarily the cause of your stress. Stay with me on this.

Whatever you do for work, that's what you do for a living. And yes, you may feel stress at work. To say otherwise would be ignoring the truth. What you need to do, however, is to ask yourself: *what am I going to do with the rest of my work life to reduce this stress that I feel comes from my work?* You can find part of the answer by observing the people who work with you. Do all of them have the same stress? I will bet there are people in your work environment doing the same thing that you are doing and that they just love their jobs. I would also bet that if your job was given to a new employee, that the new employee would be happy doing what you do. He or she would not think of your job as *stressful.*

How about stepping back for a moment and taking a good look at what you do at work. If you claim that you have a high stress job and that you are under considerable pressure at work, my first question would be: *why are you still working in that field?* Remember, you are the one that made the choice to do that work. The work did not choose you. Is it possible that you have a stressful life outside of work and are bringing that stress into the workplace? Problems in relationships, with children or relatives, can compound small problems at work and destroy your work day. Now be honest with yourself -- *are you bringing problems from the outside into the workplace?*

Perhaps you are going to say that another employee makes your job stressful. If that is the case, once again, remember that it is not the company or place of work that is causing your stress. Your stress is most likely caused by your reaction to another person. Just because that person works for the same company that you do does not mean that the company is to blame for your stress. Let's face it, some people are just not meant to work together. What do you think would happen if both of you went to work for a different company? You still have the same working relationship together. Chances are the tension between the two of you would still be the same. Thus, your stress is coming from a personality conflict, not the company.

An interesting thing about stress in the workplace is the fact that *what might be stressful to one person may not be stressful at all to another person.* Why? It has a lot to do with the particular individual and how that person interacts with other people or reacts to the particular situation or function.

Some people, knowing that the family is coming to their house for the thanksgiving dinner, get stressed-out just thinking about cooking a holiday meal. They cannot handle the necessary steps it takes to shop for the food, decorate the table, clean the house, and cook or bake the various foods. Does that mean we should think of Thanksgiving Day as stressful? Of course not. Many people love to make the thanksgiving dinner and invite as many people as they can into their home. There are so many situations in life that some people can handle beautifully, yet others claim that these same situations are too stressful. Understand that it is not one particular job or activity that is stressful. I have said for years: *stress is created by a person's attitude towards life in general and their job in particular.* Sometimes it is just the day-to-day routine and ongoing resistance to change in one's life that creates stress. Adding just one more task to the agenda may be sufficient to make some people become all stressed out while others may love the new challenge.

I always find it interesting when some report or study concludes that a particular field of employment has a high stress level associated with it. Have you ever seen a report or study that cites statistics showing that 35% of the people in a particular industry or field of work have *stress-related problems.* All right—35% of the people working in that field are stressed out! What about the other 65% that are doing the exact same job but are not stressed out? In fact, if you think about it, all you would have to do is find additional people that have the same personality, temperament, and attitude for the job as the ones in the 65% group, replace those 35% (stressed out ones) with the new stress-free group and you would have 100% of the staff in a non-stressful environment. This of course sounds good in theory but will never happen in real life.

Now I do not mean to imply that there is no such thing as stress in a job or in the workplace. In fact, a little stress in a work situation can prove to be positive once in a while, although one might feel drained as a result. All of us can get a little stressed out at times and make the statement *"my work has me all stressed out."*

When I owned my screen printing and embroidery company, I came across another business owner that was in the same business. This owner, however, was selling his business. When I asked him why he was selling his business, he said, *"my doctor told me it was too stressful a business and, to insure my health, I need to sell it and get out of this business."* What we have here are two, basically identical, businesses owned by two different individuals. While I enjoyed the type of business I owned and did not feel stressed out over it, another person in the same business is forced to sell his business because of health reasons. That brings up the big question again: *is it the business that gives the person stress, or is the stress brought into the business?*

Perhaps if you really take a hard look at your stress, you may discover that it is not coming from your job, but from your total living environment. Could it be that you are setting yourself up for stress? Let's take a good look at a typical day in the life of many people.

Monday

You get up and complain about having to go to work for another week. At work you find fault with just about everything you do and everyone connected with what you do. On your way home at night, you stop off at the dry cleaners, take in your soiled laundry and pick up your clean clothes. You get home, turn on the TV and have a beer (God knows you need one, right?). You may even take part in the preparation of the meal, have dinner with the family (don't forget the wine), and then watch a few sitcoms. The kids do their homework and maybe you help them while relaxing with a beer. Then it is lights off for the night.

Tuesday

You get up and complain again about another day of work. On your way home, you pick up one of your kids from their music lesson. The rest of the evening is a repeat of last night -- just different food.

Wednesday

You get up hating the fact that it is the middle of the week and you have to go to work. You try to sneak off early so you can catch the end of your kid's little league game, go home and duplicate the last two nights—except you eat leftovers.

Thursday

Today you get up, a little happier because you only have two days left of work. You get to work and start putting things off until tomorrow. You go home and try to eat early because the best sitcoms are on Thursday nights and you can relax with a few extra drinks. After all, the weekend is almost here.

Friday

Getting out of bed is easier because you have only one more day to the week. You go to work. You don't really feel like starting anything new or finishing up on that project that can wait until Monday when you will have a whole week to work on it. You get paid, get off of work and take the family out for dinner at a pizza, chicken, or a hamburger place. You stay up late (while you down a few extra drinks because it is Friday night).

Saturday

Today you take your kids to the little league game (hopefully your team won) and then go with the other team parents to the pizza place to celebrate the game. Afterwards, you may go shopping for food or other necessities, have dinner and maybe take in a movie with your spouse. Sometimes you may just rent a video so you can stay at home and have more drinks.

Somewhere between Friday night and Sunday night you will do the weekly house chores -- cleaning, laundry, mowing the lawn, testing the pool, fixing broken cabinets, washing windows -- whatever it may be, but every weekend you do your weekly chores.

Sunday

Perhaps you attend church on this day. Afterwards, the whole family, with the dog, get into the family SUV and off you go to the beach, mountains, desert, local swimming pool, mall, fun park, or any other place you feel like taking the family for the Sunday outing. That night, of course, you have a barbecue and a few drinks, watch more television and everyone goes to bed early because Monday starts a new week. Before you put your head down on that pillow, you grumble about having to go to work in the morning. This, of course, sets in your subconscious mind a negative thought about having to go to work. When you wake up the next day, you start the day with a negative attitude, and the exact same routine all over again for another week.

Now, I ask you, what is wrong with this picture? It

gives me a headache just to write about it. And the sick thing is, I just wrote about the lifestyle of a great number of people in this country. Many people do not realize it, but when a person falls into a pattern of repetition in his or her everyday life, just one little out-of-the-ordinary incident may ruin the whole day. In such a case, if something really out of place happens to that person during the day, he or she will suddenly become all stressed-out and may not be able to function very well for the rest of the day. When people let themselves fall into a routine, they often cannot handle change of any kind. People can become so programmed that from the time they wake up until they go to sleep, they perform only their daily routines and nothing else. If that person is you and the boss at work asks you to do something different or gives you a new task, do you suddenly stress out? If you get home and something has changed, anything at all — big or small — do you, again, stress out?

Let's focus in on one of the biggest, and, in my opinion, the most pathetic part of the American tragedy. The Monday through Friday 5 p.m. to 10 p.m. routine. Stop for a minute and think of how much of a life you really do not have in that time frame. First, you rush to get home. In doing so, you get upset at other drivers and upset that the stoplight turned red on you. If you have to stop to buy something to go with dinner, you get upset over the long line or the little old lady who is taking her time counting out change. You allow yourself to get uptight over the whole process of just getting home. Be honest with yourself, do you let the drive home drag you down?

Once you get home, what is the first thing you do? You turn on the television set. Is it really that important for you to see the news or a rerun of an old sitcom? And speaking of the news, what is so important anyway? Do you really care about some car accident that has nothing to do with you? Or a bank robbery, mugging or murder that happened on the other side of town? You are already home, so who cares about the freeway report now? Do you really have to watch that car chase that never seems to end and who knows what other great sensational stories the news media can come up with for the day. If you say you are interested in sports, turn the television on five minutes before the end of the news and you've got it. But why, and I do mean why, do you have to watch the news? There is nothing new in the news unless a major disaster hits your town. So why watch the news? You may not realize it, but the news is stressful and depressing; and you are allowing yourself to be bombarded with life's negative happenings. *Turn the television off. Next!*

Of course, after the news, you have to watch one of those tabloid news shows. How will your life change after you hear about which movie actor or actress is getting married, divorced, or sleeping with whomever? We know one thing for sure, they are not sleeping with you so why do you care? You shouldn't. *Turn that television off!*

If you think you are under stress, look at the influences that direct your life. Is that worldwide energy sucker, the Internet (Facebook, Twitter, games) draining you down each day? Talk about letting an outside influence control your life.

The first part of reducing stress in your life is to get stress-related happenings out of your life. It is so easy to do. Start by leaving your workplace a full 20 to 30 minutes after quitting time. That is right—20 to 30 minutes after quitting time. Why rush? Take it easy for a change. You just spent the day working, now relax. Let the traffic die down a bit and while you are waiting, set up your tasks for the next day. That will make tomorrow morning a lot easier.

Now drive home slowly. Stop to buy some flowers for the dinner table tonight (see Chapter One Exercise page 19). And, when you walk in the door – don't turn on the television. Leave the television *off!*   Instead, put on your favorite music and dance around the kitchen as you make dinner. If you have children who want to watch television, tell them to do their homework first and then they can watch television. If your spouse wants to watch television, just say *"I'd prefer not to watch television tonight, let's just relax."* If your spouse still wants to watch television, suggest using another television set (most homes have more than one). If you normally serve dinner at 6:30 p.m., hold off until 7:15 p.m. Go slowly for a change. During dinner and when you are finished eating, stay at the table and talk with your spouse and children about the happenings of the day.

The kids may want to jump up and leave after they have eaten, but make a deal with them. Twice a week they agree to stay at the table and tell you what has been going on in their lives. Teach them *now* how to communicate their feelings. Ask them for some input on family matters. Get them into the habit of being involved with the family and taking part in conversations.

Then have quiet time in your house, a period when everyone in the house takes some time for themselves. This is the time when your children should finish their homework, read a book or magazine article (perhaps even learn to read). For parents, it is the perfect time to do whatever they want to do without interruptions. Turn off all cell phones and if you have a landline telephone with an answering machine, turn on a message that says *"sorry, we are not taking any calls at this time - this is our quiet time."*

This is also a great opportunity to have quality family time. Get out a game, play cards, or find something in which the whole family can partake. However, no television, internet/Facebook/texting, cell phones or movies tonight. When was the last time you read a book in the middle of the week, or took the time to look through your favorite magazine? How about finding a new dinner recipe for tomorrow night? When was the last time you wrote a letter that you send in the regular U. S. Mail to an old friend or relative that is not on the internet and you can't email? Can you remember the last time you watched the sunset, the moon rise, the stars come out, or the city lights go on? I will bet that you can't even remember the last time you and your spouse (or the whole family) took a nice hand-in-hand walk around the block, and looked at the improvements your neighbors have done to their homes and yards? The idea is to relax and not jump into your old routine of television news, eat, more television, talk on the telephone, go on the Internet and then go to bed. Yet, that is just what many Americans do each and every night. Then they complain about how stressed they are.

Try it for a week and you may never go back to the old routine. Just imagine all of the great things you can do when you control your life each and every day and do not let outside forces control you. You want to take the stress out of your life? Start by changing your actions during the 5 p.m. to 10 p.m. time period each day. Take on a new attitude of incorporating *next* into your life.

How do you get away from stress? Very simple. It starts by making changes in your life. As a person under stress, you will need to work on changing your attitude about life and your perception of yourself. You will need to learn how to look at the positive instead of dwelling on the negative. Part of writing this book is to try and help you deal with your life and teach you to take that *next step*. What do you think your fate and destiny will be if you do nothing but stay on the same track you are on right now?

True Story

I was once recruited by a large company that wanted to try a new approach to helping its employees get the best discount they could on new cars. Although this division of the company occupied a five-story building, the new sales department employed only six of us and occupied a small section on the third floor. The first day on the job, I was told to show up at 8:30 a.m. I arrived in the parking lot about 8:20 a.m. I got out of my car and started a slow walk across the parking lot. I was amazed by the number of cars that came screeching into the lot, with drivers jumping out of their cars and running to get into the building. Because the building had a security guard who checked everyone coming into the building, there was a massive pile-up of people trying to get into the building at the last minute.

When I got to the elevator, just about every person on it was still getting dressed for work. I never saw so many people fixing their hair, straightening out their shirts, ties, blouses, stockings, shoes, jewelry—you name it— they were still putting on these items. When I arrived at my floor and the elevator door opened, I felt like I was at a large department store sale. The people on the elevator literally took off running to get to their desks or work areas by 8.30 a.m.

Once everyone was settled in, I observed that they were actually working and appeared to be doing their jobs. But, then came 10:15 a.m. Suddenly, people were walking all over the place and the level of conversation rose about 200 decibels; it was break time! From the rise in the laughter, sport talk and conversations about family, you would have thought that you were in the local pub. Then, after about 20 minutes, things settled down again until noon. Once again, there was this mad rush for the elevator and an increase in the noise level. The same thing happened around 2:30 p.m. But the biggest surprise for me on my first day at this new job came in the late afternoon.

It was then that we had another California earthquake. The whole building started to rumble and shake. While I started to take a dive under my desk, everyone else was making a mad dash for the elevators or stairs. One of the people I had met on my first day went cruising past me, saying: *"Jerry, it's time go home."* This was not an earthquake, it was a mad dash to get off work. I stood up and watched in disbelief as everyone was literally running out of the place. I walked over to the window and looked down at the parking lot to see people rushing to their cars. In less than five minutes the whole floor, parking lot, and most of the building were empty of people. The head of the department, one supervisor and I were the only persons left on that third floor.

I took a walk around the floor and looked at the different work spaces. I couldn't believe what I was seeing. Letters half written sat in typewriters (this was before computers) with incomplete sentences and paragraphs; and note pads with the pens lying on top of the pads looked to me as though the writers had gone to the bathroom and would be right back to finish their thoughts. Each office space actually appeared as though someone or something had come along and yanked that person right out from behind his or her desk. And, everything was very quiet. What had been a beehive of activity just 10 minutes before was now silenced.

When I got home, I told my wife that I felt so sorry for all those people that worked in this place. Obviously, it was just a job. They got paid for what they did and they delivered nothing more.

As the first few weeks went by, I met most of the people on the floor where I was working. While talking with them, I could see that for many they saw themselves stuck in a rut at work, at home and in life. It was obvious that most of them did not like what they were doing for a living and wished they were making more money. The most amazing thing of all was that they felt that they could not do any better. For that reason, they were at least happy that they had a job. And you should have heard about all the stress they were under! In my opinion, their perceived stress was self-imposed because they did not manage their time correctly and they put too much energy into complaining about their problems at work and in life, instead of finding ways to solve the problems.

Even becoming the top salesman my first month on the job, I could not overcome this negative environment. I did not enjoy working with a group of people that were down on everything and always complained about their lives, with little, if any, drive or ambition to do anything about it. In my opinion, many of them were satisfied being stuck with the jobs they had, even though they dreamed and fantasized about a better lifestyle. It will never happen for them because they don't want to make the effort to try and find that better life. They do not realize that it is up to them to take that *next step.* They did not know how to *go for it* and change their fate and destiny in their work situations and their lives. Simply put, they could not *make it happen.*

After six weeks, I decided to quit that job and get away from that negative environment. I was re-hired at my previous job where I excelled even more than I had before I left. I guess you could say I tried a double *next* that year.

Something to think about

If you told your doctor that you have a lot of stress in your life, and the doctor told you that, in less than five years you would die if you keep your job, what would you do? It is my hope that by this chapter you would say to yourself, *next*. Take the necessary *next steps* to make changes in your surroundings, and your emotional and physical well-being and *go for it*. Really try to *make it* (less stress) *happen*.

Everyone knows that stress can kill you. So why are you still working at your job or profession if you feel it is stressful? What would you say to your best friend if he or she said to you, *"my work stresses me out"?* If you are unhappy in your job and feel it is creating stress in your life but you can't find another job right now, the first thing you can do is to try your best to change your attitude about the job you do have. Don't go to work thinking about the negative aspects of your job. Try to find the positives (and there are some if you take the time to look for them). You need, however, to keep one thing in mind and that is the fact that at least you have a job. This is even more relevant today when unemployment is so high. So while you do have a job, start working on what you need to do in order to find another job.

A Few Positive Thoughts

When it comes to looking for another job, please don't say *"But I can't find any other work"* or *"I can't do anything else."* Maybe you can't quit your job today to find another job, but that shouldn't stop you from enrolling in night school or taking a correspondence course so that you can work towards a career change in the future or an advancement at your company.

Think of it as your *thing*. You can put a *no* in front of it and get *nothing*. Or, you can take *some* effort and get specific about what you want out of life. Take *some* of that efforts and put it in front of your *thing* and end up with *something*. That *something* will most likely change your life.

Why not *go for it?*

Chapter Assignment

If you have a job right now, or, even if you don't, here are some simple suggestions to help you find a better job. So grab another sheet of paper and start writing the information below.

1st: Write down your age. Now subtract that age from 18 (that would be the age you graduated from high School). That number represents your years of experience in the working world. If you never had a job in college, then subtract your age from 22.

2nd: Write down all the jobs and experiences you have had over those working years. List the things you liked about those jobs and the things you disliked.

3rd: Now draw a circle around all the positive points involved in working those jobs. Forget the negative ones.

4th: Make up a new sheet listing all those positive points and start listing the *types of jobs* that you should be looking for that possess those positive elements.

5th: Here is the best part. Because you have some years of experience that you can bring to the table, you can now go to those industries and present yourself as someone who has much more to offer that organization than someone fresh out of high school or college.

Go back to page 44 and look at what I did when I needed to identify what type of job I wanted to pursue going forward. Make up a new résumé with all the positive points you have to offer a new employer and get those wheels in motion to change your fate and destiny. Now, *go for it* and *make it happen.*

Chapter 5

NEXT–

How Do You React?

By now you should be getting the idea that one of the keys to using *next* in your life is to avoid situations that would otherwise bother you. To see if you are catching on to the concept of *next* and how you can change your fate and destiny, let's take a look at how you react to a few situations.

First, suppose that you're at home. You hear a crash and the sound of broken glass coming from the next room. When you go to investigate, you find that your children have been roughhousing and knocked over a table lamp, shattering the base into a thousand pieces. Now think—what would your reaction be?

Hold that thought for a moment and take the same scenario, only this time the family dog or cat knocked over the lamp. Now what's your reaction? Let's take it a step further, and say that your spouse knocked over the lamp. Now how do you react?

If you stop to think about it, does it really matter who broke the lamp? It's broken and it cannot be fixed. Plain and simple—the lamp is broken. Your reaction will most likely be directed towards the method in which the lamp was broken. (After all, now it - is - broken!) If the children broke it, they know that you will be upset and that you will most likely punish them. Are you going to scream, holler, rant and rave, letting this incident ruin the rest of the day? Or are you going to realize that the lamp is busted into a thousand pieces and then take a deep breath and say to yourself *next*. Make whatever appropriate statement needs to be made in a calm, cool and collected manner. Establish a punishment (no television, video game and go to your room) for the unacceptable roughhousing. And, of course, let them know how disappointed you are with their behavior that caused the lamp to break. Then make the conscious decision to say to yourself - next - and then get on with your life.

What if it was the dog or cat that knocked over the lamp? What are you going to do? Take the dog or cat out back and shoot it? If your spouse was the one that broke it, are you going to file for divorce? One of the quickest ways to assess a situation that might otherwise get you all up tight and stressed out is to turn the table on the event. Immediately put yourself in the position of the person who's the object of your anger. How would you feel and what would you expect to happen if you had knocked over the lamp?

Please keep in mind that *next* does not mean that you have to become a passive person in life. It is just a better way of assessing a situation when you keep control over your emotions. It is also an excellent method of reducing stress in your life and lowering your blood pressure.

Let's try another situation and see how you would react to it. You get into your car at the local shopping mall and, as you are about to reach the exit, you notice that there are many cars backed up also trying to leave. You decide to take a different exit. You are driving down a row of cars intensely looking at the exit up ahead to see if it too is backed up when out of nowhere a car appears right in front of you. Before you can even hit the brake --- BAM --- you hit the other vehicle. Now this is a parking lot accident. You were both going no more than 15 miles an hour. No one was injured. There was only a little twisted metal and both of you are at fault. It was a 50/50 accident. Remember, no one person is at fault. Each driver was so intent on finding that exit, that neither one of you saw the other coming from the side. So what do you do about your emotions on this one? Are you going to say to yourself "No one was hurt. Only the car was damaged and it can be fixed." Will you say *next* — and get on with your life. Or, are you going to come unglued and make life miserable for not only yourself, but for all those around you? Do you really think the people you work with want to be disturbed all the rest of the day listening to your car accident? What about your family? Are you going to explain it once and then —*next.* Or are you going to upset the whole evening by complaining all night long about your stupid accident?

How many times have you seen co-workers or relatives who have been in a fender bender make life miserable for everyone around them? They spend hours and days on end complaining about the accident which can ultimately affect you and your productivity. It is such a waste of time and energy. If only they understood my *next* philosophy. Wouldn't life have been easier for everyone if they just said *next* and moved on in life? No one wants to have a fender bender car accident. If it does happens to you, be especially grateful that no one is injured or killed. Exchange names, insurance carriers and phone numbers, then move on with your life. *Next.*

Try this one: You have to get to the other side of town. This could be for a business meeting, to buy something, or to attend a concert. It really doesn't matter what the occasion may be. You just have to be on the other side of town at a certain time. First you start off late. That, of course sets you up to be late in the first place which, in turn, sets you up for rushing. Suddenly traffic comes to a complete stop on the freeway. You are stuck between off ramps. Helicopters are flying overhead and a radio report says that a big tanker has overturned. Until they clean up the mess, you are stuck. That means you are going to miss your appointment. What's your reaction going to be? Take another look at the same scenario, only this time instead of getting stuck in traffic, you are pulled over for speeding. You get a ticket. As a result of the ticket delay, you miss your appointment. What's your reaction?

How do you react to going on vacation only to find that it rains every day you're there? What do you do when you burn the meal you made for the guests arriving in ten minutes? Nothing like having your best clothes on, walking over to your car and discovering you have a flat tire? You're on vacation and you get a call from your neighbor who tells you that your teenage daughter had a party at your home last night and the police were called?

If you really stop to think about it, when things happen over which you have no control, what good is it to let that situation suddenly control you? It happened. It's over. The damage is done, finished, complete. You can't undo something that has been done. Part of reducing stress in your life is learning to take a different approach to negative happenings around you. Focus on what you can do so they don't happen again. Then — *next* — move on with your life.

When you think you're faced with a dilemma and you are about to let it ruin your day, just imagine what your day would have been like if you had been a home owner along the New Jersey or New York shore line in October 2012 when Hurricane Sandy hit? Or if you had been visiting the World Trade Center on September 11, 2001 (9/11) when the terrorist flew planes into the buildings? Just imagine being one of the many people on one of those four planes that crashed that day? What if you had lived in Oklahoma and had walked into the Federal building at 9:01 a.m. on April 19, 1995 when it blew up? How can you complain about anything after watching the footage of that tsunami that hit the northeast coastal area of Japan on March 11, 2011. That could be you in those pictures in the newspaper that shows the "jaws of life" trying to free someone from a car in which three people died. And how many times did you drive a car and probably shouldn't have been driving. Take a second to think about that.

The point here is simple. The lamp is broken. The fenders got smashed. You got a ticket. It's raining on your vacation. You burnt the dinner. The tire is flat. Your teenage daughter can't decide if she should go join the convent or prepare to spend the next six months in her room. You can't change any of these events once they have happened, but the situations sure could have been worse. You could lose a loved one, or they could lose you. Don't let those material items, unexpected situations, or a little rain destroy your perception of life. Take a deep breath, let it all out, change your attitude and say—*next.*

Ms. Twisted Ankle

True Story: When I was a marathon runner I had to go to physical therapy for treatment of a knee injury. This was my second appointment and I was waiting with six others in the waiting room when a woman suddenly entered on crutches. Her left ankle had an ace bandage wrapped around it and she no sooner plopped down in the chair when she said, in a loud and obnoxious voice, *"this twisted ankle is so inconvenient."* We all turned and looked at her. I said, *"what happened to you?"* She proceeded to tell us how her family had gone skiing for the holiday week between Christmas and the New Year. Two days into their vacation, she twisted her ankle skiing. As a result she cancelled the rest of the winter vacation. Her husband, along with their two teenagers, had to go home. Then on top of that she and her husband had to stay home on New Year's Eve because she would not attend the annual party on crutches. She went on to tell everyone how much of an *inconvenience* this twisted ankle had become and how it was just destroying her life. This woman was so consumed with her injury that she never asked any of us why we had to be there. My first thought was *"thank God that's not my wife."*

There is no doubt that a twisted ankle will hamper your ability to go out and ski, however, it was not a broken ankle. No surgery or a cast was required, just a little physical therapy. I'm sure this mom could have lounged by the fire with her leg elevated while she read a book so her family could continue to ski. Obviously that was not the case for Ms. Twisted Ankle. I asked her if she had been here for therapy before and she said *"No - this is my first time and I just want to get this thing fixed, it is such an inconvenience."*

We all knew that this woman had no idea of what she would see when her name was called and she would go through the doors into that physical therapy room. The therapy room took up the whole third floor of a medical building and was directly connected to the orthopedic hospital next door.

I was called in first and taken to a whirlpool station. About ten minutes later they brought in Ms. Twisted Ankle. To get to the whirlpool which was right next to me she had to pass a number of patients in traction beds that had been brought over from the hospital. Some patients had rods and slings supporting their legs, some in body casts and some with exterior traction devices drilled into their skulls and shoulders. Directly across from us was a young man in his mid-twenties and we watched as the therapists were trying to teach him how to use crutches to walk, since he now had only one leg. Two stations down, another guy was learning how to lift himself from the bed to his wheelchair using an overhead bar. He no longer had any legs. When I turned and looked at Ms. Twisted Ankle she quickly looked away and sat there in complete silence.

All these patients certainly had good reasons to complain about their problems, but most displayed a positive attitude towards learning what they had to do *next* in order to continue on with their lives. On the grand scale of why people go to physical therapy, Ms. Twisted Ankle with her *inconvenience* was rendered speechless. She never said another word to any of us. It was obvious that the reality of her pettiness had caught up with her. Usually you are scheduled for the same days and times once you get into a therapy program. I had four more visits and while I saw the others from that day, none of us ever saw Ms. Twisted Ankle again.

How this event affected her home life after she left the therapy we will never know. One would hope that going forward she would feel blessed that her husband and teenagers are in fine shape and that in time her twisted ankle will no longer be an *inconvenience.*

In contrast to that story, many of you may recall the 2004 Olympics when gymnast Carrie Scruggs twisted her ankle just before her last attempt at the pommel horse. As she stood at the top of that runway all her team mates and coach stood to the side encouraging her to *go for it.* Four years of waiting for the Olympics she was not going to let a twisted ankle stop her from making that final run. It was up to her to run through the pain and go for the gold medal, not only for herself but also for the team. She took a deep breath and then took off running. Her vault and landing were a perfect 10 and the team won the gold medal. Makes you wonder how Ms. Twisted Ankle would have handled that situation.

So what has been your *"twisted ankle"* or *inconvenience* in life? When you look back over your life, how many times did you alter the activities or lives of others because of some little *"twisted ankle"* you may have had?

All of us, in one way or another, react and interact to the problems of those around us. Be it family, work or a social event, if a problem suddenly arises, how you react to that problem could very well set the tone for those involved. If you panic, the whole group may panic. If, however, you remain calm and in control of your emotions, the overall tone could remain calm. The unanswered question really becomes *"what effect will your problems in life have on those around you?"* Is the burnt dinner a *twisted ankle* and a complete *inconvenience,* or a good reason to order a pizza. *NEXT!*

Chapter 6

NEXT–

Life's Desires,

Challenges and

Opportunities

Have you ever been walking so fast that when you came to a door and reached out for the doorknob, you turned it but the door didn't open and BAM, you ran right into it! Of course you have. It has happened to everyone at one time or another. You feel stupid and look around to see if anyone saw you. Then you either turn the knob harder, give it a kick or unlock it and then walk through the doorway.

In our lives we pass through many doors day in and day out. When they do open, we don't think much about it because we expect them to open. When they don't open, we find ways around them or ways to open them. While these physical doors get us in and out of life's events and places, it is the imaginary doors of life that we must open in order to accomplish our desires, challenges and opportunities. We walk in and out of these imaginary life doors each and every day as we pass through our individual *life's situations*. The big question becomes, however, what do you do when one of life's doors won't open? Do you look for the *key* to open that door? Do you try to put a little *push* into that door of life's experiences? Do you try to find another door to open that will still get you to the same place in life? Or, do you just turn and walk away from another one of life's desires, challenges or opportunities because you don't know how to open the door?

Have you ever seen a "window of opportunity?" It, too, is much like the door. The big difference between life's doors and life's windows is that you can *see* what is on the other side of the window. Most windows of opportunity give us a chance to visualize our desires, challenges, or opportunities. We can see that dream car, the exotic vacation, better job, or the perfect mate. When we make the effort to unlatch that window of opportunity we have taken the *next step* toward fulfilling our desire, challenge or opportunity. For many, however, they never make the effort to pass through that *window of opportunity.* Many of those people find themselves standing on the *outside looking in* at all the fun others are having. While for others they are *standing on the inside looking out* at the excitement and carefree lifestyles of others. This means that the car, vacation, job, and perfect mate actually become just a fantasy. They will never experience much of a change in their destiny because they won't take that *next step* necessary to make that change. Yet with just a little more drive, conviction, or effort, you could walk through those doors or climb through to the other side of that window. You and only you hold the keys to those doors and have the ability to unlatch the windows. By doing so, you will, of course, change your fate and destiny.

You have to, however, be willing to take whatever *steps* are necessary to get those doors or windows open. The action you take is called *next* and the direction taken is called *next step.* Once you take that *next step* to move forward in life and have the desire to *go for it* and pass through those doors and windows, nothing will ever hold you back. Going further than you thought you could with any aspect of your life is one of life's greatest experiences. But it will not happen by accident. You have to set in motion a plan of action that will bring you to the other side of the doors and windows. The greatest way to do that is to take that *next step* and start setting your goals in life so you can change your fate and destiny.

I have a very simple question to ask you. What are your goals in life? Out of all the chapters in this book, this chapter may be the hardest to understand if you haven't been setting goals for yourself. *Next step* and your goals in life run hand in hand, and you need to understand why.

Without even realizing it, when you wake up tomorrow morning and get out of bed, you will have accomplished your first goal for the day. Now if you are not a goal setter, you are probably thinking, *this guy is trying to feed me a pretty big line.* If, however, you are a goal setter, then you already know that the first goal of each day is *indeed* getting out of bed. The difference between a person that just gets out of bed and a goal setter is not the function of getting out of the bed, but rather the action of how you go about the function of getting out of bed. The person who just gets out of bed without a goal usually takes his time waking up, moves that first foot off to the side of the bed, sits up s-l-o-w-l-y, stretches, and makes his way to the bathroom at a snail's pace. The goal setter however, sits up, puts both feet on the floor and is excited about taking on the day because a goal for that day is in place, and it started with getting up.

A great way to think of the two differences is to just imagine that when you wake up tomorrow you are going to have go pull weeds in the backyard or clean up the dirty dishes from the night before. Not exactly something you would want to jump out of bed to do. Now imagine that tomorrow you will be leaving early for a trip to Hawaii, or to go pick up a longtime friend at the airport. In short, if you are excited about doing something, you would be more likely to get up in the morning and move a little quicker than if you had to get up and do something you hate to do. Right? The secret, however, is to learn how to put the enthusiasm of going to Hawaii into pulling weeds or washing dirty dishes.

You may not believe this, but many people in life, and I am one of them (so is my wife), get up in the morning excited about what the day has to offer and the challenges we will be taking on, regardless of what has to be done. We have a goal for the day and we know that during the day we will be setting other goals. Some are short term and some are long term. But without those goals we don't have a focus or direction to help guide us through the day.

If you hate to get up, most likely it is because you hate the idea of going to work or your job. This of course sets the stage for you to start out your day with a negative attitude. The first step each morning is the most important step you'll take for that day. If it's a slow step then you have set the tone for your whole day. On the other hand, if you hit the floor running and you move into action for the day, you will find the whole day goes by quicker and easier.

Setting goals needs to become a very important part of your life. Goals are very important in applying *next* to your way of thinking. There are many books available on how to set goals. One of my favorite lecturers and authors on goal setting was the late Zig Ziglar. You might want to get the 25th anniversary edition of his classic See You At The Top. It is an excellent book for the person who has never set goals.

If you have never set a goal for yourself, there is no better time than right now to start putting some goals into your life. The best goal is the first one each and every morning so you can start the day with a bang. When you wake up, sit up. Take a deep breath and swing both those feet off the side of the bed. Take another deep breath, stand up and move out. Don't make getting up each morning some unwanted task. After all, you did wake up which means you didn't die in your sleep. So be happy and let's make the most of it.

Why don't you establish a goal for yourself right now? All you have to do is say (out loud) *"next - tomorrow morning I am going to sit up, swing both feet onto the floor and attack the day."*

But you don't start setting goals by just getting out of bed. Set goals for that car, vacation, perfect mate. The action that you will take to establish your goals and what you have to do in order to realize and achieve your dreams will be the ultimate test of *next*.

Remember, only one person is responsible for your life and that is the person reading this page. *Now go for it.*

Attention Parents

Many good-hearted parents have tried to help their children open those doors. Most of those parents fail when they discover that because they (the parents) opened the doors, their children never had to take on the challenges in life that are required to get to the other side. As a result of being placed on the other side by their parents these children never encountered the doors or windows in the first place. Thus, the child misses the experience of a challenge. If faced with a challenge on their own, many fail when they discover that their parents are not there to open the doors and windows.

This is played out as early as elementary school when you end up selling the fund raising candy or cookies for your child's school. Your child ends up winning the free trip to the fun park for having the most sales, yet, did not really earn the right to win. You did all the selling instead of teaching your child how to talk to people, look them in the eye and try to sell their candy.

How many parents still do all of the cooking for their teenagers and never teach them how to cook their own meals? Suddenly, they are out in the world and have no idea of how to cook an egg, let alone broil a chicken.

Your top goals in raising your children should focus on helping them understand that in order to realize their dreams in life and the many opportunities that will come before them, they need to learn how to become self-sufficient. You, as the parent, must show them how to *go for it and make it happen*. It is all part of working towards *Life's Desires, Challenges and Opportunities*.

Here is a great story. Think of your children (or grandchildren) as you read it and imagine which child you think would be yours.

Breakfast for 15

A few years ago, we attended a family get-together on a large farm in North Dakota. On the day of the big event all the parents were busy in the morning setting up tables, decorating and preparing for the arrival of many family members and guests. There were children already there but no one had made them breakfast. No one that is except our 11 year old granddaughter from California. She took all the kids, 15 of them, into the kitchen/dining area of the house and said *"I'm going to make bacon and eggs, how do you want your eggs, over easy or scrambled?"* With that she put bacon on the grill and at their request she made eggs, over easy or scrambled for all of them. Another granddaughter who was 13 looked on in amazement and said *"how did you learn how* to do that?" She replied, *"I cook at home all the time, don't you?"*

Can your child cook? Do the wash? Set the table? Sell those cookies? If not, why not! Show them the tools of life today so they can become better adults tomorrow.

"All my life whenever it comes time to make a decision, I make it and forget about it."

Harry S. Truman
33rd President USA
1945-1953

Chapter 7

NEXT–

Go Ahead,

Make a Choice

As we start chapter seven, you should be catching on to how *next* and *next step* work in your everyday life. You have a simple yet very powerful decision to make. How will your choices in life from this moment forward change your fate and destiny for the rest of your life?

If you are a person who can *read between the lines*, you know by now that one of the basic elements to implementing *next* into your life is that it is really all about choices. The choices you make each day are your choices, not those of others. One of the most important points to remember about making choices is that when you make a poor choice in something, you have the ability to make another choice to counteract the poor choice. Everyone makes poor choices in life at times. The lesson to be learned from making a poor choice is that it teaches you what to do or not to do under similar circumstances the next time. If you didn't learn from your mistakes, you will most likely make poor choices the second time around. The wisest choices produce learning experiences that lead to better choices in the future.

When the alarm goes off tomorrow morning, what choice will you make? Will you continue to lie in bed and take your time getting up? Or, will you make the choice to *next* the day and go for it? When you get to work, will you continue putting things off that need to get done? Or will you choose to *next* them? When you come home tomorrow night, will you choose to keep the same old dinner time habits? Or, will you choose to *next* the evening and try some of the suggestions outlined at the end of chapter one. All of the choices are up to you. Will you choose to make positive changes in your life? Or, will you continue to make the same mistakes over and over again, keeping your fate and destiny on the same track?

Everything you do in life boils down to choices. If you are not happy in a situation, be it work, love or play, it is because you are making choices that keep you unhappy. Sometimes being unhappy is just an easier way to deal with life than to make a choice to change something.

When someone hits "bottom," he or she has a choice. Stay down there as long as he or she wants, or make the choice to start the climb back up. Amazingly, many people want to stay at the bottom because *it's easy.* Climbing out of that hole can be overwhelming for people who have not discovered how to tap into their inner strength. Thus, they choose to stay at the bottom and remain weak.

Did you ever watch an interviewer talk to people that just went through a disaster? Some people reflect the attitude that, because of the loss and devastation, his or her life is over. Others will say: *"well, looks like we'll have to pick up the pieces and just start all over again."* Or they may say: *"we may have lost all of our belongings but we still have our family. We'll find the way to get back on our feet."* Take a moment and think of what your reaction would be if you lost it all? What words would you use to describe your feelings? How about *next?*

Making choices seems so simple, yet for some people, making a choice seems like a life and death decision. Is anyone holding a gun to your head and holding you to your job? Are you going to make a choice and do something about your work situation? Or, are you going to just stay where you are? If you find you are not having fun anymore, choose to move on in life. Find some other form of fun. It's out there, you just need to put in the energy to find it. One thing is for sure. Whatever that "fun" thing may be, it will not come looking for you. You need to go find it.

Choices. It's that simple. Now *go for it* and *make it happen!*

A FEW FUN THINGS TO DO

➤ Hike a trail or ride a bike along a bike path

➤ Go to Alaska and see the last frontier

➤ Join a book club

➤ Look up at the stars at night instead of the TV

➤ Go camping and sit by a nice campfire

➤ Call up an old friend and just talk about life

➤ Write down the history of your family tree

➤ Write that book that is hiding inside of you

➤ Learn digital photography

➤ Take a vacation in an RV

Great spirits have always encountered violent opposition from mediocre minds.

Albert Einstein
1879 - 1955

Chapter 8
NEXT-
Visualizing

The mind. What a wonderful instrument in life. Whereas our brain controls our physical actions, our mind offers us so much more. It is our mind that affords us the opportunity to learn, understand, reason and find our purpose in life. It allows us to re-live our past and plan our actions for the future. We form our opinions, beliefs, and desires in our mind. *Visualization* allows your mind to look ahead and actually see yourself doing something different or accomplishing a goal.

It is no secret that some of the highest achievers in sports, business, and the arts actually use visualization to see themselves achieving their respective goals They see themselves crossing the finish line first, making it to the top, or completing a certain task as they train, study, or work towards achieving their goals. It is important, especially in *next*, not to confuse visualizing with fantasizing. Although I have nothing against fantasy, and everyone I have ever met fantasizes at one point or another in their lives, the big difference between visualizing and fantasy is that a fantasy is nothing more than a wild desire or notion. Most of those fantasies remain unfulfilled because they are unrealistic.

How many people have fantasized over owning a $250,000 sports car, a vacation home with a large yacht moored to a dock at a luxurious yacht club, a home on a hundred acres of land with horses and a big lake? These are fantasies when one does not have the income to obtain them and no plan to acquire that income. Granted, if you work hard and make enough money so that you can afford those items, your fantasies can become realities. Most fantasies, however, remain fantasies and never come true. Remember, we live in the real world and unlike a Disney movie, life is not a fairy tale. With visualization, on the other hand, you know that if you put what it takes into action to reach that goal, it will become a reality. Before anything takes place, however, you have to have the desire to *go for it*. Sure, you can fantasize about doing or achieving anything. But can you visualize yourself taking on all the work and responsibility necessary to really get there?

Watch out however, as you need to keep your visualized goals within reach. Don't let them flip over into fantasy. Visualizing yourself as a great guitar rock and roll star when you haven't even learned how to play the guitar would be a fantasy. If, however, you have untapped talent and you learn to play the guitar, join a local band and hire an agent, you will have started the process to becoming a rock star. If the agent obtains a contract for you to tour with a major group as the opening act, your destiny will change. Because everything is in place for you to visualize yourself as a rock and roll star, you could make it a reality.

For many, visualizing can be a form of role playing with the mind. For example, if you ever had to confront someone, how many times did you first play out in your mind, over and over again, what you would say? You visualized how you would handle yourself and what you would do if a certain event happened? That is not fantasizing, that was visualizing the upcoming event.

Visualization is another important aspect of *next* and *go for it*. The more you visualize, the better prepared you are to take on any challenge life has to offer. Just because you visualize something happening one way, when in reality it turns out another way doesn't mean that you wasted your time visualizing the event. It just means that you have to *next* it for right now and get on with your life. Don't let visualization take over your life. Everything in life will not turn out the way you visualize it. When you know what you're trying to accomplish, understand the challenge and set your goal, visualizing your success will help to make it a reality.

One of the best statements about visualizing I ever heard was made by Tiger Woods in 1997 when he won his first Masters Golf Championship (earning the "green jacket") at the Augusta National Golf Club. He was handed a microphone after donning his jacket that evening and asked to say a few words. The first thing he said was, *"I visualized winning a Masters, but I never visualized what I would say when I won it."*

Before you fantasize about winning the Masters Golf Tournament, change your fate and destiny right now by visualizing yourself doing a better job in your field of work, or the way you relate to your family and friends and your future. Then *go for it*.

The only reason some people get lost in thought is because it's unfamiliar territory.

Jim Fixx – Author/Runner
(1932-1984)

Chapter 9

NEXT–

Thoughts, Ideas and Inspiration

Everything presented so far plays an important part in helping you understand how to *next* life's situations in order to change your fate and destiny. Teaching yourself how to capture thoughts, ideas and inspirations is a powerful instrument in learning the secrets of how to *go for it* and *make it happen!*

Thoughts and Ideas

Think for a second of the number of times a thought or idea spontaneously popped into your mind. For example, there you are at work doing your job when suddenly you get an idea on how to solve some problem. Maybe you're at home preparing dinner when a great thought comes into your mind as to how you could get two things done at once tomorrow while you're shopping. No matter who you are, what type of work you do, where you came from, what you look like, how old you are or what sex you are, all of us are bombarded with thoughts and ideas each and every waking hour.

In fact, we have thoughts and ideas while we are sleeping, only we refer to them as dreams. Just because you think of something or see yourself doing something, but you happen to be asleep, is no reason to discount that thought or idea. If you want to say *"it came to me in a dream"* that's okay. What would you call it if your thought came to you while sitting at work? Would you say *"it came to me while I was daydreaming?"* Have you ever been talking with a friend and suddenly something they say triggers an idea or thought, even though it is not related to the topic of the discussion? The bottom line is very simple. It really doesn't matter if you are sleeping, wide awake, or engaged in a boring conversation. When a thought or idea hits you and you learn how to capture it, you need to take that *next step* and act on it. If you do, you may just see a dramatic change in your life.

Just look at the history of our country over the last 100 years. Countless thoughts, ideas and inspirations that were implemented have changed the way we live today. Do you realize how many of the things surrounding us started out as someone's thought or idea? God did such a wonderful job of creating our earth and everything on it. He gave us the ability to develop thoughts and ideas through communicating skills, writing and speaking. While we can strive for a life above the basic needs of animals and learn how to reason and make choices, God gave us the ability to take thoughts and ideas, and develop them. As a result, we are able to lead a more comfortable life than those before us.

Do you enjoy your car, television, microwave oven, cell phone, air-conditioning system, computer, iPod? These began as thoughts— ideas— and look what happened? Stop for a moment and realize the changes that have taken place throughout the total existence of mankind and you'll realize that all those changes are the results of someone's thoughts and ideas turned into reality. They became reality because someone took that *next step* and had the mind set of *go for it* and *make it happen* by acting on his or her thought or idea!

This doesn't mean that, if you can't come up with something that is going to change the way we do things in life, or you don't have the money to make some new items for the marketplace, your thoughts and ideas are not valid ones. Your thoughts and ideas, as they pertains to you, are valid. The key, however, lies in your ability to capture them.

A fellow Toastmaster, Mr. Gene Siciliano, once told an audience, *"when it comes to thoughts and ideas, you better write them down right now; because once they're gone, they may be gone forever."* If you teach yourself how to catch them by writing them down, you will never lose them.

How many times have you had a thought or an idea that you didn't write down or act on it immediately? Within less than a few seconds, you can't remember what that thought or idea may have been. If someone suddenly calls your name or engages you in conversation, chances are the thought or idea you are entertaining may disappear and never come back. This happens to everyone. You might say, *"well, why not just remember it?"* The answer is easy. Thoughts and ideas are not part of your conscious memory bank. That's why they are not called memories but thoughts and ideas. Some people believe that you have those thoughts and ideas stored in your sub-conscious mind and, like butterflies, they just suddenly flutter into the conscious mind. If you don't act fast, they just flutter away.

Those that believe in the wisdom of universal knowledge will tell you that everything conceivable is a thought that is *out there*. To have the ability to tap into that source of knowledge through meditation, intuition, or any higher state of mind can heighten your awareness to your surroundings and guide you along in life. No matter how a thought or an idea comes to you, when one does come along, take the obvious *next step* and write it down. Capture it. When you look back at what you wrote, you may find that the thought or idea could change your day, week, year, or even your life. To be inspired to act on the thought or idea is the ultimate *next step*.

Years ago, before I started writing down my thoughts and ideas, something would pop into my mind, and then I would become distracted and I didn't write it down. The idea was gone. For the life of me I couldn't remember what it was. Many times I even forgot that I had a quick thought or idea. Weeks later, I would get the thought again and realize that if I had put the idea into practice the first time, I could have saved a lot of time in what I was working on last week. As a result of getting a time saving idea, and then losing it, I started carrying those little ring-flip note pads with me wherever I would go. There is one in my jacket, my car, at my desk, in my briefcase, and next to my bed. Wherever I am at or whatever I am doing, when I get a thought or idea, even when it has nothing to do with what I am doing right at that moment, I take that *next step* and write it down. For a long time I carried a small voice recorder but now I can just talk into my cell phone. I transfer those notes or recordings to my computer at a later date.

Did you ever see one of those note writing devices with the big black suction cups to put on the dashboard in your car? I could never understand why people bought those things — until I bought one. Many ideas come to me while driving my car. To be able to just pick up a pen, jot down the thought or idea while I sit at a stop light, or pulled off to the side of the road, assures me that the thought or idea has been captured. Have you ever been driving down the street when you see something happen, or the action of an individual walking along the sidewalk suddenly generates a thought or idea? Many times a topic for a speech at my Toastmasters

Club, or a way to convey a message to someone at an upcoming meeting, came to me because I wrote down something I saw or heard on the radio while driving. Today, many people have all sorts of apps and voice activated systems on their cell phones that can help them capture their thoughts, ideas and inspirations. Whatever and however you choose to do it is not the issue. The issue is setting something up so your ideas don't *flutter away.*

Taking the small notepad concept a step further, you can move it into the workplace. In every business I have owned, I place a large ringed note book right alongside every telephone at the work stations or desks. Every time an idea came to anyone's mind, I told my employees to write it down in the book. If an employee talked to a customer on the phone and the caller asked questions, I instructed my employees to write down any thoughts or ideas the customer may have expressed to them about getting a job done. At the end of each day, I would review the books with the employees. There, in those books, were not only the names and numbers of the people they talked to, but the thoughts and ideas that the employees had while talking to them. We may not have put the thoughts or ideas into use right at that time, but down the road many of those thoughts and ideas became very valuable to the success of our back room production.

While attending a Chamber of Commerce monthly "mixer" meeting, the business owner of a sign company came up to me to say *"Thanks for that great suggestion of placing notepads around my business. We have gone back to those books many times to look for the thought or idea we had while talking to someone on the telephone. That was the best business tip I've been given in a long time."*

A lot of the contents in the chapters in this book and in my other books *IT LOOK EASY! IS IT? Simple Steps for*

Small Business Success and *PROSPECTING – PRESENTATION – CLOSE, Your Three Keys to Successful Sales* are from different thoughts and ideas that I jotted down in notepads in my car, at work, and at home. Making the commitment to write those books is a great example of taking that *next step* and putting it to work. Sitting down to actually write the books, finish and publish them changed my fate and destiny. Writing this third book is another *next* for me and represents my continued desire to *go for it* and *make it happen!*

Remember, ideas are like those butterflies. If you don't grab them right now (write them down), they could be gone forever.

Inspirations

In a basic sense, you have two forms of inspiration. The first type comes to us as a thought or idea. You think of something or have an idea. You start putting energy into the thought and suddenly you're inspired to take some form of action. Everyone, at one point or another, has been inspired by a thought or an idea. It is the second form of inspiration, however, that usually comes to us via some outside source or a second party. We see something take place or hear something that just overwhelms us. We feel inspired for that moment to take some form of action. We take this action either on our own, or, because another person told us what to do. It is from these outside inspirations that most people take the most action. This can be as simple as watching some activity or observing the behavior of another person that may inspire us to take action. If you act on your inspiration, you will have taken that *next step* on your part. However, you would have never acted upon it had you not seen something on your own, or been inspired by someone.

Second party inspirations usually come to us

unsolicited. Many times we fight off the opportunity to be inspired. For instance, a friend convinces you to go with him to listen to someone speak on a subject that is of interest to him. You really don't want to go, but end up going anyway. When the speaker is finished, you find that you are even more inspired by what the speaker had to say than was your friend. How many times have you seen a movie and were inspired to take up some sport or activity? These type of inspirations usually generate more of a *go for it* attitude than if a friend tried to get you to do something new.

In 1989, while watching the Los Angeles Marathon on television, a reporter interviewed a young man who had been an alcoholic and hit bottom the year before. I remember his interview and how he said that he had watched the L.A. Marathon while in a rehabilitation center. He said, *"I saw all these people, healthy, fit, and running in this race. I looked at myself in the mirror and thought, 'I'm going to do that next year."* And sure enough, he did. Watching his interview, I was inspired by his ability to get his life in order and take on that challenge. Here I was, a runner for close to 15 years, and I had never run a marathon. In short, he inspired me to take the marathon challenge. That next year I ran the L.A. Marathon. I ran that Marathon five more consecutive years after that. The interesting part of this story is the fact that I had watched the L.A. Marathon ever since it first started in 1987. Why didn't I run it then? I was never inspired until I heard that fellow talk about overcoming his drinking problem.

A positive inspiration of any kind, if acted upon, will change your fate and destiny. The key phrase here is *acted upon.*

Word of Caution

Here is one word of caution when we talk about being inspired by someone. There will be times in your life when you will cross paths with people that may inspire you for the moment. Step back and evaluate that inspiration properly. Don't act on anything that could cause harm to you or to others. Someone who encourages you to break the law, destroy property, or harm others or yourself is misguided even though they may have the ability to inspire. For example, in the jungles surrounding Georgetown in Guyana South Africa is a place called Jonestown. It was there that Jim Jones moved his People's Temple congregation from Ukiah, California and on November 18, 1978, 913 American citizens, 276 of which were minor children, all lost their lives in a mass suicide plan. Parents seeking God actually gave poison punch to their children first and then all the adults proceeded to take the poison. Everyone died in that "revolutionary death." Jim Jones apparently killed himself with a gunshot to the head. It is hard to believe that anyone would follow the command of another to commit suicide. You have to wonder, also, how one man could convince 637 people to give their children poison and then drink it themselves.

Then there was Marshal Applewhite. He was the Heaven's Gate cult leader who in the spring of 1997 convinced over 30 members in his group that a flying saucer trailing behind the Hale-Bopp comet would take them to heaven. In order to gain admittance onto the *ship,* they needed to shed their earthly "containers." They ate poison-laced applesauce and then covered their heads with plastic bags. News reports stated that they found people with purple-cloaked bodies and wearing brand new Nike shoes. Indeed, misguided inspirations.

Why are children picking up guns, making bombs and attacking their fellow students in schools across the country? Could it be misguided thoughts, ideas and inspirations? Some say movies, video games and music are to blame. Other think it is a lack of parental guidance. Some blame society. Many times there are no clear answers to what causes a young person to kill another. There is no doubt, however, that the young person came up with the idea of what to do and something (or someone) inspired them to follow through with their actions. It is key, whenever possible, that we understanding their motivation for their misguided actions so others can learn from their mistakes.

Whatever your thoughts, ideas and inspirations may be in life, focus only on the positive ones. Learn how to become a better person, friend, employee, parent, spouse, son or daughter. When you can achieve clarity in your intentions you will help make a better life for yourself and for those around you. Once you have that plan for moving forward in your life, that is the time to *go for it* and *make it happen!*

Stop being concerned with something over which you have no control. Instead, take control of the events in your life that should be of utmost concern to you, such as family and friends.

Jerry X. Shea

Chapter 10

NEXT—

Life Isn't Fair

How many times have you heard someone say. *"That's not fair?"* What is fair anyway? Is it fair that some children in this world grow up with clean clothes to wear, food to eat and stay nice and warm in winter with a roof over their heads, while other children, born on the same day have little or no clothes, go hungry much of the time, and have no place to stay warm in the winter? Is it fair that one person gets cancer and dies, while someone else gets to live? What is so fair about standing in line to buy tickets to a concert and you end up with seats that are in the last row, but the guy ahead of you got seats right up front? What is so fair about a brother or sister that can do no wrong and the one time you step out of bounds everything goes wrong?

The answer is simple: *life isn't meant to be fair and there are no guarantees in life.* After all, life is full of challenges. Some turn out right for you and others turn out right for someone else. Some of life's challenges don't even make any sense to you and can seem very unfair at the time. No one can guarantee anything about life. When you fall for the attraction of a guarantee in a life situation, you are just opening the door for a big disappointment. Life isn't always fair.

Fair does not seek out good or evil, right or wrong, moral or immoral, justice or injustice. What may be fair to one person could be unfair to another. Many things happen each day that involve the question, was that fair or unfair? If you are one who always says *"But that's not fair,"* you need to learn how to deal with the big picture of life (see chapter 11).

I don't mean to suggest that when you see something that you feel is wrong you should ignore it. Not by any means. But at the same time, don't spend your life living on the *that's not fair* wagon. Don't let a *that's not fair* situation destroy the rest of your day. Take the *next step* and get on with your life.

A great example of looking at fair.

One morning as I was about to go for a run, I received a call that a relative had been taken to the emergency room at the hospital where I worked (see chapter two). After I arrived at the hospital, I found out that he had what appeared to be a stroke. He was now down in the Cardio-Vascular Lab undergoing tests, in the very lab where I worked for 12 years. I stayed with his wife for a while, but until the tests were over and he came back to the room, there was really nothing I could do. I told his wife that I would check back later and went off to my office. Once there, I discovered a large envelope on my desk. This was not just any envelope. It was from the budget committee, the very committee that four years earlier approved the expansion of the Hospital's Department of Education and my transfer to it from that Cardiology Department. There was talk that the hospital administration had changed its original plans to expand the Department of Education and this envelope would confirm or deny the rumor. When I opened the envelope up my heart sank. The Budget Committee rejected my budget for the expansion of my department. There was no doubt in my mind that the plans for expanding and growing our department had been rejected. The day had just begun and already things were happening all around me that did not seem very fair. The handwriting was on the wall. My job was being phased out. I was very upset and decided to go home and take that morning run that I didn't get to take earlier in the day.

It was about 11 a.m. when I arrived home. My wife was at work and the kids were in school. Since I was unable to run that morning because of my unexpected trip to the hospital, I decided that this might be a good time to do so. I had been running for a few years and running always relaxed me. I put on my shoes and shorts and took off for a nice five-mile jog.

As I got about one-half mile down the road I suddenly heard a loud screech. I then felt sharp points on top of my head followed by huge bird wings flapping on both sides of my face. I ducked quickly as I kept running. I turned and looked up to see what hit me. I saw nothing. As I kept looking up I heard that screech again. Out of the sun came this big bird, wings stretched out as it dug its claws into my scalp, again flapping it's wings onto the side of my head and then taking off again. A little dazed and confused, I found myself in the middle of the street with cars stopped as the drivers watched a large hawk continue to attack me.

Suddenly a police car pulled up and gave his siren a quick blast to get my attention. The policeman reached over, opened his passenger door, and yelled *"Jump in."* I ran to his car and dove into the front seat just as he hit the gas and we pulled away. As I sat up he said, *"She's a protective one. She must have a nest in the trees right above you."*

He turned his police car around and gave me a ride back to my house. I put some antiseptic on my hawk cuts and stood there looking into the mirror thinking, *"why me? This is not fair.*" I just wanted to go for a run. What was happening with this day? What else could possible go wrong? I decided that maybe the best thing to do would be to just lie out in the sun and get some rest. This would keep my mind off of the direction my day seemed to be going.

I was relaxing on my back basking in the warmth of the sun when suddenly something heavy, gooey and smelly slopped right onto my chest with a big loud *SPLAT*. My eyes popped opened just in time to see this huge seagull flying overhead. That's when I realized what he had just dumped the biggest, gooiest mess you could ever imagine right there on my chest. This constipated bird must have been eating dead fish and rotten sandwiches from trash cans for over a week and it finally let loose! I jumped up and leaned over the patio fence and let this wad of goo slide off my chest and into the bushes below. I looked up again and realized that there was only one seagull in the whole sky. And there he was flying away, slowly gaining altitude. I ran inside and jumped into the shower. After a very heavy soaping and long rinse, I stepped out of the shower, looked into the mirror again and thought - *"What is going on here? This really is not fair."*

The department's budget is cut and I know I'm going to lose my job. I'm attacked by a hawk while trying to run. And then Jonathan Livingston Seagull decides to take a dump on my chest. Let's face it. What the day had to offer was far from fair in my opinion. Then again, to what was I comparing "fair" for that day.

The gist to this story goes back to what had happened earlier that morning. That "relative" in the emergency room wasn't just any old relative. It was my father. I received a frantic telephone call from my mother telling me that she thought he had suffered a stroke. It turns out that when my dad woke up that morning, he could not move the left side of his body from head to foot. Luckily, he was taken immediately to the hospital .

This was the type of situation every son or daughter anticipates they may confront one day. I was concerned for the health of my father and tried to comfort my mother. The doctors wanted to run some tests and let him rest. My mother wanted to stay right in the hospital room so she could be there when he came back from the tests. That was when I had decided to go to my office for a while.

So who was having an unfair day? Compared to my dad, my day was a walk in the park. For my mom, she was sitting there facing uncertainty and life sure did not seem fair to her. Fortunately for my dad, what appeared to be a stroke at age 64 was really a concussion resulting from hitting his head on a door jamb as he got into a small car the night before. He recovered, and lived a good life until 89.

To step back and analyze the events of that day is what really makes this story interesting. Let me break down the events of that day as I see them today. Keep in mind that this happened over thirty years ago when I was in my late thirties. Also, my understanding of life was not as advanced then as it is today.

First, not knowing that my dad had hit his head, and thinking that he had indeed suffered a massive stroke, made me furious. He had been a smoker all of his life and all the years I had been a cardiac technician, I kept telling him he had to stop smoking and he didn't. To me, it was the smoking that caused his stroke and I was very angry at him. The more I thought about it, the angrier I got. What if he died? My mom would be alone at age 62 because my dad refused to give up smoking. I was so angry at him that you could cut my anger with a knife. I needed to get away from that room and that is when I decided to go to my office.

When I got to my office and saw that the administration

had declined my department's budget, I also realized that my position was being eliminated. This was disappointing and added to my anger. Angry at my dad and disappointed in the budget, I just wanted to get out of there. I went to my dad's room and told my mom I was going home for a while and would be back later to hear the results of his test. I left the hospital and my mom sitting in the hospital room alone waiting for my dad to return from his test. While running I am attacked by the hawk protecting her nest. And, with all the sky above and all the ground below, a seagull pin-pointedly targets just my chest!

When you look at the series of events happening so close together, one has to question what was really happening that day? Was the hawk really protecting her nest? Or, was that some kind of a force that was trying to stop me from running so that I would pay attention to my dad who was in the hospital? Since the *powers that be* failed to get my attention the first time with the hawk, was the seagull guided by that same power, once again, to try to get my attention? Were they trying to get me to stop thinking about myself (anger) and my job, and to realize that I had left my mom alone in a time of her need? Was the budget rejection part of an over-all plan to help me move on in life? (which I did). Did any of this really have anything to do with fair or unfair? Why did I view these events as unfair when I should have seen them for what they were really all about - signs from above trying to get my attention? Sometimes I jokingly state that if I had not snapped out of *my self-pity* after that seagull dumped on me, the next thing that could have happened was for me to see a *burning bush*. And for the record, I went back to the spot that the hawk attacked me and there was no nest in the trees or any hawk to be seen – hum?

Obviously, I should have stayed at the hospital to help support my mom. My thinking at the time was that my dad was in good hands with the very people with whom I had spent twelve years with in the Cardiac Lab. and until all the test results came in, there was nothing I could do.

Instead of comforting my mom as I should have, I let my anger at my dad and my emotions over the budget get in the way of common sense. Not exactly a high point in my behavior.

The moral of this story is to realize that everyone goes through times in their lives when they feel life isn't being fair to them. But to what are you comparing "fair?" More importantly, I realized on that day that there are times when some outside force can try to get your attention. It has nothing to do with fair or unfair. In fact, a situation or event that you may consider to be "unfair" may be a sign from above.

What would you rather have happen in your life: a parent suffer a stroke or you get a pink slip?

The more you understand how important it is to just *next* all of the life situations, even those that may seem "unfair" to you, the better are your chances for not getting stuck on hold. Believe me, I have looked high and low and I cannot find anything that says life is supposed to be fair. So why waste time on something you view as unfair? Take a second to evaluate it (in case it is a sign from above) and then move on with your life. Learn to develop a positive and optimistic outlook on everything around you. Stop being concerned with something over which you have no control. Instead, take control of the events in your life that should be of utmost concern to you, such as family and friends. Focus on the direction in which you are trying to move and stop wasting time on thinking life is unfair. Keep moving your energy forward. You accomplish this by continuously taking the next step and learning how to *go for it* and *make it happen*.

"No matter where you go you can't get away from yourself, so you'd better make yourself into somebody worthwhile."

Anonymous

Chapter 11

NEXT—

The Big Puzzle of Life

At some point in your life, you have most likely heard someone say *"Life is a puzzle,"* or *"That's one of life's puzzles."* They made a reference that life is made up of a lot of pieces (like a puzzle), or you don't know the answer until everything (the puzzle) is put together and is complete.

In understanding *next*, the analogy of life as a puzzle is really a great one. Just think of the puzzle of your life as a whole bunch of little puzzle pieces that are already put together and represent your life right up to this moment. You cannot change the pieces in this puzzle as what has happened in your life has indeed happened. It was your fate and you can't change it. The unplaced pieces in your puzzle of life represent your *next step* in life going forward. Your ability to choose the correct pieces, the ones that will help make you a better person and help create a better picture in your puzzle of life, will come down to the choices you make when you *next* life's situations. Only you can determine if you should *go for it* and make those changes in your destiny.

I want you to take a moment and visualize a large—very large—and unique puzzle on a wall that goes from in front of you, all the way to your left and completely out of sight. It is a puzzle made up of trillions and trillions of pieces. Within this puzzle are billions of smaller puzzles all designed to create that one big puzzle (picture) that some refer to as *The Puzzle of Life*. When you visualize this imaginary big puzzle (picture) of life, you can see everything that has happened since the beginning of time. All the religions, social activities, ethnic groups, the environment, everything that makes up our life on earth is before you. All the events and happenings that took place all these years are in that puzzle. Directly in front of you are the images of the world for today, with everything that happened yesterday just a little to the left. To the right, however, there is nothing. Nothing because we have not reached tomorrow.

What makes this puzzle so unique is that each of us has a section in this multi-trillion piece puzzle that is being filled in with the puzzle of our own life right up to this very moment. Because each of us (in the imaginary sense) will view this puzzle of life from our own perspective, there, directly in front of you, is your space in this puzzle of life.

Life, if you really stop and think about it, is nothing more than an ongoing puzzle. The things you do each and every day are made up of small little pieces in your daily life's puzzle. Then, at the end of your day, that composite of small pieces that has created a day in your life is placed in your section of the big puzzle of life. In reality, the things we do each day and the fact that we have influences on other people (and their puzzle of life) shows we actually do contribute to the total puzzle of life itself. While you helped to create the big puzzle (picture) of life you are also trying to figure out how that completed puzzle of *your* life will turn out. You can see what you have already done in life because those days are over, and of course they represent your fate. Go ahead and take a moment to really visualize your puzzle of life. Can you see your childhood and some of the things that you have done in life? What about those teenage years? Do you see a few pieces in that puzzle from that time in your life that you would love to take out permanently and forget? Sure there are, but you can't take out or undo what has been done. How about that first job or your first real job after your education? If you take the time to visualize your puzzle of life you will see all of the days and years leading right up to today and this very moment.

What is so interesting about this puzzle is that each and every day of your life all the un-placed pieces, laying all around you on the floor (symbolically), can eventually be moved into each day's composite of the puzzle. Depending of course on your choices in life, everything that you know of, and some things you are yet to discover, can end up being placed in this puzzle. Each day that your part of the puzzle is completed, it will not represent a particular picture, but rather a unique composite that is a reflection of your life. You can see your challenges, accomplishments, successes, failures, and everything that happened in your life that created the end result — *you.*

What is not complete in your puzzle of life is from this very moment forward. In other words your destiny. Imagine that before you on the floor are thousands of pieces of life's puzzle representing everything that life has to offer. Many of these pieces are designed to help you become a better person. Some represent new and exciting things for you to do or try. A few, however, are self-destructive, immoral, harmful, negative or toxic pieces. Some pieces can even affect other pieces of the puzzle in the life of someone else. Now here is the important catch to these puzzle pieces. Although everything that life has to offer is in those pieces on the floor before you, you can't just pick them up and fit them into your puzzle *unless you are willing to make the commitment that goes with each piece.*

These pieces of life's puzzle, yet to be placed, represent the ultimate in your ability to take that *next step* and change your life. You and only you will determine how the pieces will go together and what your final big picture of life will look like. You must ask yourself *"what kind of changes will I make from this point going forward (destiny)?"* Most important of all, *"what will I be doing with the rest of my life to determine how those pieces fall into place (fate)?"* Making those life altering changes will be your true test in taking that *next step* and your ability to *go for it.*

Remember, your puzzle (picture) of life fits into the big puzzle (picture) of life itself. What you do in life and how you do it will, in many cases, enhance or alter that big puzzle/picture. When you choose to do something that has a positive effect on someone else or even a group of people, then that act not only enhances your part of the puzzle but the lives and puzzles of others. When you choose a destructive action, however, one that can affect many others, that choice will not only change your puzzle in a negative way, but create a negative piece for many others.

Did you ever hear the expression *"everybody is someplace, somewhere?"* Where you are in life, right now, may not be the place you want to be, however, there you are. As I stated in chapter one, you are not someplace else, you are right here. Look at that puzzle, and there you are. You have spent your whole life getting to the point you are at right now. Let me ask you a very important question— *"Do you like the place you are at in your puzzle of life?"* If your answer is yes, then good for you. That means you know who you are in life and where you're going. It should come as no surprise, however, that many people have a slight desire, or maybe even a major drive, to be someplace else in life. If you look carefully, you will see the places in your puzzle of life that have allowed you to get to the very spot where you are right now. After all, you do have a place in life and you are indeed *in it right now!* If it's not the place you want to be, both physically and emotionally, then it's time to take that *next step.*

When we talk about being where you want to be there is much more to it than just the physical placement of your body. You have to include the emotional (mind), spiritual (spirit) and physical well-being (body), which are far more important than the placement of your physical body.

Remember, *"everybody is someplace, somewhere."* The real answer to being where you want to be, is to know that you are comfortable with your life, feel good about what you have accomplished and look forward each day to becoming a better person. You have a desire to be more knowledgeable, better adjusted to life's changes and eager to learn more (mind). You have an inner peace about you that makes you comfortable in life (spirit) and you take good care of yourself with a healthy diet and exercise (body).

Don't confuse your physical location with your emotional, spiritual or physical well-being when you hear the phrase *being where you want to be.* Going to the dentist may not be one of the places you want to be, but it is just one of the placements we find ourselves at that are necessary in order to function in life, or in this case, have healthy teeth and gums.

We are going to take a quick look at where you are physically in just a minute. More important than your physical placement, we need to look at your emotional place in life, examine your spirituality, talk about that body of yours and discuss your ability to take that *next step.* With that unfinished puzzle in front of you, you will have the opportunity, at this point in your life, to change your fate and destiny.

Having said that, we need to understand how each of us plays an important part in creating the overall picture of who we are and how we fit into the life's puzzle of the world we live in. To do this, we do have to look at our physical place of being, but only for the purpose of helping us identify where we want to go *next*.

Do you think you have a place in life? The answer is very simple. Yes! You do have a place in life and you are in it right now! If you don't like this place, you have the unique opportunity of picking up the pieces to your puzzle (life) and starting over again by taking that *next step* to a new life situation. It's that simple.

Let's define being where you want to be from the physical standpoint. Wherever you live and whatever kind of neighborhood you live in may not be the place you want to be physically. But if you think you would be much happier living in a mansion at the top of the hill, or in a large home on some oceanfront property, and that is your great example of where you want to be — think again. It is not a good example at all. Your physical placement in life, up to this point, had a lot to do with many personal events that took place in your life. Your parents, your education or lack of education, type of job you selected, type of income you created for yourself, and many of the changes that took place in your life have created your placement in life. Some of which you may not have any control over, but all of which have brought you to the physical placement you are at right now. Knowing that, what are you going to do to change your physical placement? It is up to you and only you to make that change. Don't rely on someone else making that change. This one is up to you. Are you ready to take that *next step* and change your physical placement? Before you jump to "yes" you need to evaluate just one thing. Could it be that you don't need to change your physical placement at all, just your emotional placement of yourself?

What you may really need to focus on is your emotional well-being and how that has brought you to the place you are right now. Your emotions control just about everything you do from the time you get up until you go to sleep. Some people are in touch with their emotions and know how to control their behavior. Many people, however, let their emotions run wild and those emotions end up controlling them. Remember that sadness is an emotion just like happiness. When we are happy, things seem to go right. When we are sad, things tend to go wrong. Staying happy is another key to *next step* and your success at keeping your emotions in check.

Your spiritual side (not religion) of this puzzle is one that will reflect how much you are at peace with yourself. Spirituality is really a universal power which all of us can tap into. Some find that power very easily and have a great spiritual awareness within them. Others have never even tried to tap into it. Your *next step* to a better understanding of spirituality is to go to the book store and look at all the books on the subject. These books are not there by mistake. If you have never looked in that section of the bookstore before, you are in for a big shock when you see how many books have been written on spirituality. Learning how to tap into your spirituality and wisdom will turn out to be the biggest *step* you will ever take and something you should not put off. After all, before you on the floor lie all the pieces of your puzzle for spirituality. All you have to do is pick them up and place them, however, without some knowledge and guidance the pieces will not fit.

As for that body you have? Yes, that is your body and as many folks say *"this is what God gave me."* The big question then becomes *"Are you taking care of that body the way God wanted you to?"* In chapter two of this book I outlined the importance a good healthy body plays in your overall health. Please review that chapter and try to understand it.

This brings us to the last important pieces of the puzzle. The pieces that represent your future. Before you are pieces for religious beliefs, pieces for where you will be physically, pieces for your home, family, friends, your work, your goals in life, and the most important pieces of all, the ones marked *next step*. These, above all others, contain the means to a happier, healthier and even a more prosperous life. The key to seeing these pieces lies within one's conscious and subconscious mind. For it is there that you and only you can control your emotional (mind), spiritual (spirit), physical well-being (body) while having the ability to take that *next step* in your life and *go for it*.

When you look at your puzzle and realize that you have the absolute power to change the future events in your life, are you going to make some changes or just stay on the path you have been following? Are you ready to take on new challenges? Would you like to place some of those pieces into your puzzle of life and end up seeing a new you?

We can all remember being a child, so let's go back in time to your thirteenth birthday. Imagine that before you is a gift. It is wrapped. You take off the paper, open the box and find a completed puzzle that shows how your life will turn out, right up to the age you are at as you read this book! When you see what your life will turn out like, you are amazed at some of the things you are going to do. Especially some of the *stupid* things you are going to do in life. You want to take those pieces of the puzzle out, but you can't.

Now come back to this very moment and remember your life from thirteen up to the present. Now that you really know the complete story of your life up to this point in time, there are probably pieces of the puzzle you don't even want to look at or be reminded of. In fact, if you really could go back to being thirteen again, would you want to change pieces of the puzzle so your life, going forward, would have turned out differently? Well, we can never go back, for what has happened up to this point in our life is over and done with, and those pieces of the puzzle are in place. After all, those pieces of the puzzle are what have made you the person everyone knows as *you*. But guess what? We sure can make changes going forward in life.

What changes, in your mind's eye, would you make that would take your emotional level to a new high? How would you address your spirituality? And what changes would you make to your body? To realize the power that you possess over yourself is greater than any man-made power on earth.

No one, and I mean no one else, controls those pieces that are you. When you really come down to it, when nothing else matters or when everything matters, what you do, how you react, what you say, what you believe, and how you handle yourself will all be a reflection on your puzzle of life. That is a true statement about life. The question is, are you willing to make some change in your puzzle of life or are you going to pick up that one great big piece marked "nothing changes" and place it in your puzzle for today, again tomorrow and each and every day after that?

I fully believe that anyone is capable of making positive changes in their life no matter what their age, their up-bringing or their present situation. Unfortunately many people go for the *nothing changes* piece of their puzzle instead of reaching for the *better health and a happier life* pieces. They choose to pick up the piece marked *buy lotto tickets* instead of *save for financial security*. They reach for the ones marked *drugs and alcohol* instead of *stay sober*. They kick aside and step over the ones marked *life challenges* or *take a risk on something new*. All those new exciting pieces of their life's puzzle lay before them and they reach for *nothing changes*. If those folks would just say the word *next* and start picking up new pieces for their life puzzle, life as they know it today could change dramatically and provided them with a positive life for tomorrow.

Are you ready to change your life puzzle? There is no better time than right now to make a conscious decision to set some new goals, take a risk on something new and your first step towards a new you. So take in a deep breath and as you let out that air say real loud—***Next.*** Then take that *next step* by picking up some new pieces of your puzzle, placing them in your puzzle of life with joy and excitement and then start *going for it* and *making it happen.*

Our self-image and our habits tend to go together. Change one and you will automatically change the other.

Unknown

Chapter 12

NEXT—
Are You Afraid of YOU

Think back to when you were a child. I'll bet that you remember someone asking you to do something physical, such as cross a bridge, climb a tree or dive off of a diving board, and your reaction was "I'm afraid." You were afraid you would get hurt. After all, you had never tried it before. You may have had visions of falling and breaking your arm, or even worse, killing yourself (most likely implanted by your mother). There is also a good chance that in time, be it a few minutes, hours, days or even years, you tried doing whatever it was you were afraid of, and you did it without harming yourself. In fact, you enjoyed it so much you did it over and over again.

Also as a child, you may have been asked to do something that was not physical, but it required more of an emotional effort, such as getting up in front of the class and giving a speech, or being on stage in the class play. Again, you may have reacted with fear. You were probably afraid that your classmates would laugh at you. Or you may have been afraid of making a mistake, being misunderstood, forgetting your lines, or merely scared of standing up in front of people with all whose eyes and faces looking back at you.

Are you still afraid as an adult? Most adults assess very quickly if death is a possibility when attempting something physical. Unless someone is trying to talk you into catching a bullet with your teeth, you will have to admit that you probably will not die trying something that thousands of other people are doing every day. Statistically, if you take lessons in sky diving, or in mountain climbing or underwater scuba diving, there is less of a chance of dying than being in a car accident on a holiday weekend.

The larger question is, "are you still afraid to try something new?" Is the thought of making a mistake, being laughed at or not being perfect keeping you from moving forward with your life? You must ask yourself: "what is it about *me* that makes *me* afraid of *me?* If there was ever a time to think of taking that *next step* to try and *go for it*, this is the time.

One of the greatest things in life, one that gets you excited and gives you a reason to jump out of bed in the morning and makes you feel as if you have something to accomplish that day, is to wake up with a desire to try or do something new. Once you have the mind set to try something new, all kinds of magical happenings take place in your life. Because you have elected to take that *next step*, you have automatically opened the doors to meeting new people, seeing new sights, and most important of all, experiencing something new.

For many people, however, taking that *next step* is a very difficult one and they need to move slowly. In order to accomplish this, some people need to start slowly. For them, they may need to test the waters and get their feet wet. They must feel that they can enjoy it before they take the plunge.

Many people are "stuck in life" and walk around with a cloud of doom and gloom hanging over their heads because they are afraid of themselves. To them, making any change would be changing the person they think they are. For that reason, they cannot see any change in their fate and destiny. All these people need to do to get out from under that cloud is to allow themselves to step out into the sunlight. You accomplish this by making a change in your mental attitude and exterior image. It starts by feeling good about yourself and putting a smile on your face. Nothing does it better than wearing a different outfit to give yourself a new look.

To kick start that first change of events and to help put a smile on your face, we need to dress you up. We need to get you into some new clothes. Your first step is a change in your outward appearance. Just as the quote states on the page before this chapter, *"Our self-image and our habits tend to go together. Change one and you will automatically change the other."*

Everyone can remember a time in their lives when they dressed up for some event. I am talking about really dressed up. When you did that, you felt very polished. You most likely looked in the mirror and liked what you saw reflecting back to you. You had to admit that you looked pretty darn good. It put a smile on your face and gave you an inner warmth. You felt good about yourself. Wherever you went that day, other people commented on how nice you looked. Well guess what? It's time to get dressed up again.

Now you don't have to keep checking your mailbox for an invitation to a black tie affair; and you don't have to go out and buy a whole new wardrobe. Just find in your closet or shop for one item you like to wear that makes you feel good when you wear it. If you're a guy that hates to go shopping for shirts and pants, how about looking for a new casual jacket, not an everyday work jacket. Go to a specialty shop and find a sweater or sweatshirt jacket. How about a jacket with your favorite sport team name is on it? Buy a cap,

T-shirt, vest, anything that's a little different from the way you normally dress. If you are a woman, take a chance on buying something a little out of character from what you would normally buy. I'm not talking about buying clothing for work, but purchasing a really nice casual outfit for the weekend. Buy something that you may have always wanted but never bought. The point here is for you to take a little risk on buying some clothing and to feel good about it. If you are short on cash right now, stop in a second hand store, the Salvation Army or a thrift shop. Go wherever you can to find something that is new for you. Put it on, wear it with pride and while you are at it, put a smile on your face. Feel good about yourself and your choice in clothing. After all, we are talking about *you*, so look sharp and be happy.

By the way, should someone tell you that he or she doesn't like what you are wearing, just tell the person, *"I'm not wearing it for you, I am wearing it for me."*

Let's look at what will happened. By simply purchasing new clothes, you changed your fate for this day. One simple act created a change that otherwise would never have happened.

Do you understand the power you possess to change your destiny by changing one small event in your life? Just one simple change and look what happens. You will end up helping the economy with your purchase. You will now look a little different. But most important of all, you have taken charge of your own actions and became an active player in the game of life.

What would happen to you if you made a number of changes in your life? How about the fact that you would be changing your fate and destiny?

Think you're too old to change?

In the early 1980s, my wife and I went with some folks to

Acapulco for a vacation. My wife's mother, Hilda, who at the time was 66 years old accompanied us. The hotel where we stayed offered the famous parachute ride, one in which a power boat pulls a large parachute behind that has a seat for a person to sit. The power boat pulls the parachute until it lifts to a height of the tallest hotels. The view from high up in the parachute seat is spectacular and ever-changing as the boat pulls you around the bay. The only sound you hear is the wind blowing past your head. It is one of the closest sensations to "flying like a bird" I have ever experienced. It is quite an exhilarating experience.

After I took the ride, my mother-in-law said, "I would like to try that." The takeoff and landing point was a small barge in the bay. Hilda took off without touching the water. When she came in for a landing, she landed right on the platform, which was better than landing in the water which I did.

Later that evening around the hotel pool one young man was talking about his parachute ride. It was amazing that so many older people would say, *"You got to be crazy to go up in that"* or *"You'll never catch me going up in one of those."* One man in particular was sitting on the edge of the pool with his feet in the water. He was in his 60s, overweight, not in good physical shape, and had a fresh thoracic scar down the middle of his chest. Turns out he had undergone open heart surgery six months earlier. He spoke negatively to anyone who talked about their parachute ride.

The contrast between that guy and my mother-in-law was like night and day. My mother-in-law, who knew she would not be killed riding the parachute, took the risk and enjoyed a part of life that this poor guy and others like him missed during that trip. Makes you wonder how many of life's other exciting adventures people miss and continue to miss in their lifetime. By the way, Hilda lived to be 86 years old and always enjoyed telling the story of her parachute ride.

You may not need to take a parachute ride to make a change in your life, but you do need to do something that changes your everyday routine. There are two great old sayings—*"Spice is the variety of life"* and *"No one is as tired as the person who does nothing."* So what are you going to do to spice up your life? What changes are you going to take to start doing something differently with your life at work, at home and socially?

The choice is yours. You can be an observer of life's happenings as you stand off to the side and watch others take part in the fun activities. Or you can join in and become a participant in life's happenings. *Next* is the only action statement you have to say to yourself so you won't be afraid of *you*. Now *go for it* and *make it happen!*

A few exciting things to do in life
(I have done all of these – you can too.)

- River running with an organized river running company.
- Horseback riding.
- Kayaking on a river, lake or the ocean.
- Weekend trip to a National Park or campground.
- Hike a local trail.
- Put on a set of rollerblades/roller-skates.
- Go bike riding.
- Drive two hours away from home for a Sunday brunch. (Go one way and return another way).
- Get a massage.
- Go to a coffee house with a new book. Order a drink you have never had before and sit down and read the book.
- Bring your lunch to work and go to a park to eat it.
- Volunteer to pass out water at a 10K run.

- Check your community activity calendar and go to a weekend event.
- Buy a cookbook and try a new recipe.
- Learn photography and how to work a digital camera.
- Attend a computer class and learn more about the Internet.
- Discover the fun of computer graphics and start making your own cards (use the photos from your photo class).
- Go see a movie that you think you would not like to see. You just might be surprised how much you liked it.
- Rent a boat on a lake and go fishing
- Go see Alaska
- Order something on the menu you have never had
- Volunteer for a political campaign (It is a lot of fun)
- Enter a 5/10K walk/run – just walk it if you don't run.

While the above list contains activities anyone can enjoy or get involved in, here are a few things I have done that are a little outside the box:

- Photographed a river running expedition down the Omo River in Ethiopia, Africa (1973).
- Toured half the USA on a motorcycle long before motorcycle touring became popular (1979).
- Wrote this book while traveling in a motor home (will have visited all 49 states when trip ends in 2013).

The idea here is to just find something new to do and start making things happen in your life. Now *go for it.*

"Once you make the decision to move on, don't look back. Your destiny will never be found in the rearview mirror."

Mandy Hale

Chapter 13

NEXT—

No ifs, ands or buts about it

While growing up, my mother would tell me to do something that I may not have wanted to do. By the expressions on my face, she would follow it with *"and no ifs, ands or buts about it."*

There is absolutely nothing that anyone can say that is more distant or 180 degrees away from a *next* than the statements *"but what if..."* or *"yeah but..."* People who have not learned how to incorporate *next* into their lives will constantly fall back on *"yeah but"* or *"but what if"* when asked to do something different.

When someone says *"but what if,"* what are they really saying? The answer is one of two things. One, he or she is comfortable with the way things are and want to continue their life without any changes taking place. After all, in order to makc a change in what you do, it means you will have to take a *risk*. And, that *risk* may or may not turn out the way you want! That makes the *risk* a threat to what you have been doing and with which you are comfortable So you put it off with a *but what if*. Second, in order to take the *risk* you have to make a decision. *But what if...* and *yeah but...* people have a difficult time making decisions because they fear what could happen if they made the wrong decision.

Before people can change anything in their lives, they definitely have to drop the *yeah but* and *but what if* attitude. Learn how to replace it with a strong conviction of *next*. How much of a *yeah but* and *but what if* personality you may have, I don't know. For the sake of this chapter, let's look at what happens to the *yeah buts* and *but what if* people in society.

People with chronic *yeah but* and *but what if* personalities can't decide if they should stand, sit, walk, run, talk, keep quiet, turn left, turn right, look up or look down. They fear that whatever they decide to do will be the wrong decision and/or something negative will happen to them. Everything in their lives revolves around *yeah but* and *but what if*. They have an inherent fear of change in anything they do. For that reason, they may never really change much of their destiny. Actually, their destiny in life is really their fate. Since they can't change fate, fate becomes their destiny.

We all know people that live the *yeah but* and *but what if* lifestyle. It is so sad to see a person that cannot grab life by the tail and give it a good swing. *But what if* I buy the present and she doesn't like it? *But what if* I order the chef's special and it doesn't taste good? *Yeah but* if I paint the room a new color the curtains may not match? *But what if* I buy that shirt and find out it doesn't match the pants I have? *But what if* I ask for a date and she say "no?" *Yeah but* if I accept the date I may not enjoy the person and have a lousy time? *But what if* he asks me to marry him, what should I say? *Yeah but* what if I buy a new car and someone steals it? *But what if* I *make* a suggestion and my boss hates the idea? *But what if* I tell them what I really think and they don't like me anymore? *But what if, yeah but, but what if, yeah but, but what if?*

But what if you die tomorrow? Is that a reason to stop living for today? If you are a *but what if* person, you will never make much of a life for yourself until you understand that the opposite of *yeah but* and *but what if* is *"go for it."* In order to *go for it* you just have to learn how to take that *next step* to *make it happen.*

The exciting step in making *next* work for you is to take those *risks* in life. Life without risk is like a car without gas --- you're not going anywhere. The person that has spent his or her life always starting each sentence with *yeah but* or *but what if* has had a hard time taking a risk on almost everything they have done in life.

Now I cannot expect you to suddenly change and just drop that *but what if* attitude. Start small. Try just one new thing (anything). If you attack it with a *go for it* and *make it happen* attitude, it will be your first step in breaking away from your old *yeah but* and *but what if* habit. By taking a small risk you will realize that your life won't end and that the sun will still come up tomorrow. Amazing things will begin to happen in your life if you learn how to think *next* and keep moving forward. You may find, for example, that it is okay if someone returns a gift you purchased. You made the gesture to give a gift and that is what was important. *Next.*

Do you realize how many people took a risk to make this world a better place to live? Everything that surrounds you right now happened because someone took a risk. Someone had a positive attitude and decided to *go for it.* Nothing happens to anyone who starts a project with *but what if?*

In order to put *next* to work for you, you will have to eliminated the *"yeah buts"* and *"but what ifs.* When you catch yourself starting to say *"yeah but,"* shut your mouth, think it out, and say "Lets go for it" instead.

There is little chance of ever getting ahead if you are a skeptic, negative thinker, or a person who is afraid to put a little risk into his or her daily life. It's time to enjoy the chef's special, get new curtains for the repainted room, buy that new car, present your idea to the boss, and go out on that date and just have a good time. Take the risk. *Go for it and make it happen! Next.*

More persons, on the whole, are humbugged by believing in nothing, than by believing too much.

P.T. Barnum

Chapter 14

Understanding the

Boundaries of NEXT

In this chapter you will understand that by using *next* when faced with any of life's situations and taking that *next step,* you will move forward with your life instead of settling in on one of life's dead-end streets.

When you encounter one of life's problems, move forward *(next)* and away from the problem. Why? Because, just for right now, this very minute, you can be more productive if you move on to something else. Get back to the problem, dilemma, or situation later, Put off the problem to another time, if you can, a time when you can put more energy into it or have the chance to think it out more fully. *Next* means "move on" and stop deliberating over something over which you have no control right now, can't change (if at all), or can't seem to resolve right at the present moment.

When you *next* a situation, you find that in many cases you end up with a better solution to the problem. This is because you have taken the time to first think it out. Sometimes you may also find that the situation has worked itself out without your help. Time may have changed the original situation. The problem may have just gone away without incident. The people that presented the problem worked it out for themselves. Whatever the problem or situation may have been, it no longer exists. Think of the frustration and anxiety you have eliminated from your life because you remembered *next* and how to use it.

In emergency and life threatening situations in which quick and immediate action is required, such as a car accident, fire, earthquake, tornado, or flood, always take the *next step* immediately and become a person of action. Do not be the person who just stands there, doing nothing. Remember, *next!* The accident happened, the fire started or whatever the emergency situation may be and someone has to take action. Call 911, help the injured people or do what you can to help out. When you *next* this type of a situation you are not moving away, but using *next* to assess the situation and get involved.

There is no doubt that life is a road of many valleys and peaks. Strive to always be moving forward when you are working towards a goal in life. Recognize those dead-ends and *next* them by going in a different direction while keeping your spirit and attitude moving forward. Remember, life is too short for anyone to just keep driving straight without taking a few exciting turns in life. Also keep in mind that it is okay to pull over once in a while and take some time to *smell the roses and watch the sun set*. When it really comes down to it, life will always go on with or without you. It is just too bad that you may miss out on so much of what life has to offer because you didn't learn how to take that *next step*.

If you find yourself traveling down a road that seems to be heading for a dead-end, turn around. Go back the way you came and find another road to travel. Should you stay on that dead-end road, you will find yourself with thousands of others that have given up on the experiences and joys life has to offer. They settled for compromises that are far less satisfying than what they could have had if only they would have learned how to take that *next step.* Keep a mental picture of the word *next* in your conscious mind. Say it out loud every once in a while. Keep moving and always make an effort to *go for it* and *make it happen!*.

The past is but the beginning of a beginning.

H.G. Wells

In Part Two of this book we will review different aspects of life. You may relate to some of them. They will hit home for you. Others will remind you of family, friends or co-workers.

Part Two

NEXT—
Go For It and
Make it Happen!

Death is nature's way of saying "Howdy."

Chapter 15

NEXT—

You're Gone

There are many things that this book has to offer you that can help you establishing a more successful, prosperous, happier and healthier lifestyle. The one thing that this book, or any other book cannot tell you is when your moment of death will take place.

Death, after all, is inevitable for each and everyone of us. Even a person who is going through the process of dying does not know exactly when he will die until that moment comes. One day, each of us will travel through that *tunnel of bright light* to reach the other side.

Everything about *next step* deals with our life as we live it on a day-to-day basis. This book has been written to assist you in making your life more exciting, help you recognize your potential, and keeping you from a life that is *stuck on hold.*

Learning to work with fate and destiny, as it pertains to your daily life (see chapter one), is your ongoing challenge. While traveling down that road of life, however, should your ultimate fate/destiny find that you have been "called up," (your number's up, you bought the farm, your time's up, you get the call, end of the line" or any other cliché you care to pick) then you have fulfilled your purpose on earth. If you believe in life after death, as I do, your spirit is now needed elsewhere.

If this sounds strange to you, and you are not familiar with the relationship between your body and your spirit, or you have doubts about what will happen upon your death, then you should talk to your clergyman. Read books on the subject and even attend seminars on *life after death*. After all, the very last *next step* for all of us on this earth will be death. If you take the time to understand what life is really about and accept death as a part of that life, you will discover that death is nothing more than a fraction of the experience of life itself. You will also observe that people who accept death as a part of life have a peace about them that those who fear death do not have. I have witnessed this in the military, the hospital setting, and in people all around me. In fact, I find that many people who fear death fear life also.

But you are not gone yet. With death in mind, however, and for the purpose of this chapter, we are going to assume that you are indeed *dead*. You died a few days ago. Your life is over—finished—the end. Now let's look at what you have left behind.

First of all, did you have a life insurance policy? If you answered *yes*, good for you. I just hope you increased the face value of the policy as your income and standard of living increased. If on the other hand you never took out a policy, or had one and purposely dropped it or stopped making payments on it, then I sure hope you died without a spouse, children or any type of family. If you left loved ones behind without financial security, you were irresponsible or not a caring person. Who would depart from this world and leave loved ones financially strapped? In this day and age, while you are raising a family, both husband and wife should have life insurance policies. Just because one may be a *stay-*

at-home person is no excuse for not having life insurance. If you do not have life insurance, take that *next step* today. Ask a friend for a referral to an agent or company that can go over your options on life insurance.

Now that you're dead, your family has set next Tuesday aside to read your Last Will and Testament. You do have a will don't you? Oh no! You don't have that either? Do you know how disgusting it is to watch your family members and relatives fight over your belongings? Do you realize the devastation you've created for your son? He really wanted to have that little pocket knife you bought for yourself on that great family vacation you took a few years back? You know, the one he likes to borrow once and a while? The one that reminds him of the hike the two of you took that afternoon when everyone else wanted to stay at the hotel and watch a DVD? And now look what's happening. Your spouse didn't realize how important that little pocket knife meant to your son and she just gave it away to charity along with some of your other personal items. Is that what you really wanted to have happen to your keepsakes?

And look at that fight over your old music record albums. We both know that if anyone was going to get your great collection of old music records, it was going to be your longtime best friend. After all, long before you were ever married, the two of you were buying those great hits together. Who better to get your copies of the great hit songs that always reminded you of that double date the two of you went out on in high school? But look, your brother's wife just took the record collection! Is that what you wanted to see happen after you're gone? The point here is very simple. It is time to take that *next step* and get your Last Will and Testament in order. After all, those possessions of yours are going to end up somewhere. Just because you're dead and can't take them with you is no excuse for letting then get into the wrong hands or creating problems for other people.

Now there is absolutely no excuse for this next one. In the last 24 hours did you tell anyone, and I mean *anyone*, that you loved him or her? Did you say *I love you* to your spouse, children, parents, relatives, best friends? In fact, let's not worry about the last 24 hours, how about the last week, month or even year? Here you are dead and gone, and all these people can't remember the last time you told them you loved them. Take the *next step* with this one on a daily, weekly, and monthly basis. Give loved ones away from home a call once in a while and be sure to say "I love you" before you hang up. Stay in touch with friends and remind them of how much you appreciate their friendship. Most important of all, give immediate family members a daily hug and tell them you love them. Remember, once you are gone, they can never feel your embrace again.

And now for the really big question — did you die *happy?* Did you do those things in life that you said you were going to do? As the saying goes, "did you do everything on your *bucket list*" or, did you keep putting them off and now look what happened? You're dead and now you'll never get to do them. Too bad, too. I bet you would have really enjoyed that exotic vacation you always talked about taking with your spouse. And what about that fun trip you wanted to take with your kids. You know the one that was just like the fun time you had with your parents when you were young. Those were such great childhood memories for you. Too bad your kids won't have them. Then again, when your spouse remarries, maybe that new partner will take them on that fun trip and the memories will be connected with your replacement. Is that what you want to have happen also? Did you ever hear the expression *"Life is too short?"*

There is a great book written in the 90s by Stephen M. Pollan and Mark Levine called *Die Broke*. When you are finished with this book, get their book and read it cover to cover. Mr. Pollan, referred to on the book jacket as "America's most trusted financial advisor," writes about what you should do with your money as you earn it, save it and spend it. The most important part of the book is his (and my) philosophy that you should enjoy spending your money on you, not work hard to pass it on to others through an inheritance. Mr. Pollan feels that you should let your kids and grandchildren *earn* their *own* place in life and society. It is really sad to think that people are waiting for you to die so they can get your money. Why not spend it on them now? That way you can see them enjoy it. While you are at it, why not go ahead and spend your money on things that you can enjoy now? Take that exotic vacation or buy something which you have a right to buy with *your money.* If the beneficiaries of your estate get upset because you are *spending their inheritance* — too bad. Spend *your* money on *you* and enjoy life. Let your children and other relatives work hard for their money just as you did. Read Mr. Pollan's book. It is a *next step* to a whole new way of thinking about money and your life.

There are so many other things you should have done before your untimely death. But wait a minute – *you're really not dead yet.* Well that's a relief. That means you have time to take that *next step* right now. You *can* put together that will, start planning that exotic vacation, arrange that trip with your kids and all the other things you always wanted to do. And what do we have here? Is that your red sports car parked out front?

My mother-in-law used to say *"I never saw a U-Haul following a hearse to the graveyard."* That is another way of saying *"You can't take it with you."* So don't be one of those people who is always saying *"I'll do it next year."* Make the time *now.* Stop putting things off in life and start *living life.*

Remember, tomorrow may be another day, but there are no guarantees you'll be here to enjoy it. So before you are really gone for good, start enjoying life and take the attitude of *go for it* and *make it happen.* Do it today.

Note to Reader: Spending your money in an irresponsible way is downright foolish. You should spend your money wisely, not on lotto tickets. Make sure you plan for the future and save for retirement. Once you have met your yearly financial obligations (including future obligations) then you can decide how, where or to whom you want to spend your discretionary money. Once retired, you will need to budget your spending because you will be on a fixed income (combination of your saved retirement income and Social Security). There are no bonus checks in retirement.

Should you decide to *spend a little of your money on someone while you are alive* I would like to hear about it. A great way to encourage others to do the same is through testimonials. My mailing address is on the front cover page.

Chapter 16

NEXT–

Get a Real Job

Many people may feel the need to have some *power* in their life, especially in their job. Unfortunately, many of these people do not realize that the true power they are seeking is actually right inside of them. Each of us possesses so much power with our own abilities that there is really no need to *display* to anyone that you have a *powerful position* or have *power over them.* In chapter 22 you will read about two different people of power, but for this chapter we need to discuss your abilities as it relates to your job.

Did you ever stop to realize how much real power you possess in the workplace? You have the power to climb the ladder of success and go as high as you want to go. You can choose to be the best you could possibly be in whatever job you are doing. Assume you made it to the top, became the top dog - the BOSS - then you would suddenly discover that you are standing at the bottom of yet another ladder. The new challenge when you are at the top of one position is to move up to the next level. Will you take the challenge by changing companies for an opportunity to move up even higher on a new corporate ladder? Perhaps becoming the boss at a larger company or starting your own business. Once you make the conscious decision to *go for it*, nothing should stop you.

Now saying to yourself *"I want run a Fortune 500 company"* when you haven't even held a management position is a little unrealistic. To say you want to start college, get into an MBA program and go to work for a Fortune 500 company is very realistic. Provided, of course, you truly intend on following through with it.

But you don't have to have a goal that strong to succeed in life. As I related in chapter four, if those employees had put a little more effort into their work and had viewed it as more than just a nine to five job, they would have been setting themselves up for more success and achievement in their work environment and for themselves.

We all have to have a job of some kind in order to bring in the money necessary to live in our society today. After all, unless you are living in the mountains or off of the land, you need money to buy basic necessities and some of the luxuries of life to which you may have become accustomed.

Just because a person needs some type of employment is no excuse for having a poor, unsatisfying job. Unfortunately, some people perceive themselves as being unable to get a *decent* job and just settle for whatever job at whatever pay rate they can get. They never try to improve themselves or put any effort into moving into a better paying job. That, of course, never stops them from complaining about their job. This is where *next step* comes into play.

First, if you really can't pull yourself together enough to improve your education, advance your skills, or change something that would help you get a higher paying job, then *stop griping about the job you have!* Be thankful that you have a job in the first place and start working on your attitude so you can start enjoying your work. Don't make a job your hell, make it your haven.

Secondly, look at your options. Believe me you have many. You can start by signing up for night school or a trade school with evening or weekend classes. Increase your basic knowledge by attending a one day class on a subject you like. Talk to friends about their jobs and what they like about them. Find something, anything, that might be of interest to you and learn more about it. Remember who is in control of your destiny? It's *you.* So start doing something to change that *dead end path* your traveling on and start changing your destiny by taking that *next step* and *go for it.*

True Story: I once had a young employee who was not very happy at his job. Although he was a good worker and was at the top of his pay schedule for that job, it was not enough to cut it for all the debt he had incurred. He saw little or no future ahead and viewed his job as a dead end. He started to develop an attitude problem, had family concerns at home, and his world was falling down around him. One day he got into a fist fight with another employee. After talking to both of them, I gave them both a second chance and did not fire them, although I had plenty of cause to do so.

About four months later he got into a fight with a different employee and this time I fired him. Getting fired was the best thing that ever happened to him. When he thought about getting another job he realized that no matter what company he worked for, he really wasn't happy in that field. He ended up enrolling in a government funded training program, learned a new skill, and went to work for a company that started him off at over $6,000 dollars more a year than he was making with us.

His story is a great example of being forced to take that *next step.* Although the events for a career change were forced upon him, he had no choice but to move on to another career. He took the necessary steps to make a change in his life and that proved to be very beneficial and changed his fate and destiny.

But here is the real *kicker* to this story. If that employee had been able to leave his personal problems at his door step and go to work *for* my company each day, instead of going to work *at* my company, he could very well have advanced to a very prominent position with higher pay without having to change careers. But youth, inexperience and an uncontrolled temper, fueled by personal problems at home, kept him from seeing or understanding the potential for advancement in the position he had.

One of my favorite stories about a person's relationship to his work is the one that Zig Ziglar told about the two guys both going to work for a railroad company on the same day. Twenty years later, one of them is the president of that railroad, the other is a supervisor. When asked by another employee how the supervisor knew the president, the supervisor replied *"We both started work on the same day, I went to work for $2.25 an hour, he went to work for the railroad."*

So here is the question for you. Are you working for the company, or just working for a few dollars an hour? Maybe it's time you said *next* and did something about your relationship with your employer. Better yet, why not just *go for it* and show your employer that you are the best at what you do? Who knows, better things may come along when your employer realizes you're working for the company and not just for a paycheck.

Now go for it and make it happen.

How can you find your fortune when you cannot find yourself.

From the song: *Sit Down Young Stranger*
by Gordon Lightfoot

The dread of loneliness, being keener than the fear of bondage, we get married. For the one person who fears being thus tied there are four who dread being set free.

Palinurus,
The Unquiet Grave

Chapter 17

NEXT--

Relationships and

Dating

If there was ever a subject where *next* plays an important part of your life it has to be when you are *dating*. Actually, the word *dating* should be dropped from the dictionary and the correct word for going out with someone should be *personality testing* or *PT* for short. Let's face it, what you are really doing is checking out the different characteristics, mannerisms, and personalities in different people so you can determine the type of person with which you want to spend the rest of your life.

Before some young person reading this says to him or herself *"Not me, I'm just dating to have a good time and party."* Well guess again. Would you go out with someone you can't stand? Or better put, would you have a fun time with someone who has nothing in common with you and is the *date from hell?* Of course not. Even though you may not be dating with the thought of getting married to anyone, you should still be dating different people as you try and figure out what you like and don't like in a relationship. At some point in your life you will most likely plan to spend the rest of your life with *someone*. You sure better know what you like and don't like or it will be a short lived relationship.

Unfortunately, many people latch on to the first person who comes along because they are afraid of moving on and taking that *next step* to find the right lifelong mate. I could write a whole book on the experiences of people who rushed into marriage and those that waited until they met the right person, but we'll save that for another time. For the purpose of this chapter, I bestow upon you one simple task, and that is to take part in a quick test to find out what you are looking for in a lifetime mate.

In order to do that, please take a piece of paper and draw a line down the middle. On the top left half write the word *likes* and on the top right half write the word *dislikes*. Now, under *likes* write down the qualities in a person you would like to have in the ideal relationship. Remember to write down only the qualities in someone's personality. Don't write down rich, extreme good looks, famous or fancy car. Those are just material things and have never been the grounds for a strong relationship. Also write down the things you enjoy such as types of movies, music, foods, style of clothing, everything that elicits a response of joy when you hear it, feel it, or see it. Write down the types of loving behavior you would like directed towards you, but don't confuse loving behavior with seductive behavior. Passion and sex are just that -- passion and sex. You may want a mate that likes to seduce you, but just read the books on marriage (or surf the Internet) and you will discover that as the years move on sex will not take up that much of your life. If you can maintain an active sex life for 25 years (let alone 50 years) you will be way ahead of the majority of married couples. You do want to list loving behaviors including holding hands, hugging, kissing hello or good-bye, buying a gift because you want to do so (not because you're expecting something back) and dinner by candle light (in your own home). These are what some romantics call the *touchy feely* gestures without going for sex.

On the right hand side of the paper, list all the characteristics you don't like about someone and the things you don't enjoy in life. This could include a person that is always complaining, takes life too seriously or not seriously enough. Someone who is uptight or too laid-back. Conservative or liberal, atheist or born-again-Christian, sloppy or overly tidy. Just keep listing habits, actions, and personality traits that you don't like. Also include things that you don't enjoy. Playing bingo on Thursday nights, hanging out at bars, a particular type of music or movies, foods you don't like to eat. List all the things that bring the opposite of joy when you hear, feel or see them. ***Make the list right now.***

I want you to take a good look at the paper. What you see before you are the good and the bad qualities that you are looking for in a mate. We both know, however, that there is no such thing as the perfect mate or someone that will have 30 out of 30 *likes* on your list. If you found someone with 22 out of 30 *likes* then that could be someone to consider for a lifetime relationship. Saying you are in love with someone with 4 out of 30, I don't think so. What you really need to focus on, however, are the qualities of a person you listed on the *don't like* side of your list. This side of the list contains the traits that will really kill a relationship if you don't recognize them up front.

This list is now your road map for dating. If you meet someone and feel you are attracted to them physically, throw out a few of your *likes* as you talk to the person and see how they respond. Before you even get to the point of going out on a date get their input on the things you have on your *don't like* list. For example, if you were to say *"I just love hot spicy Mexican food,"* and the person you are interested in says *"I hate hot food, my stomach gets all upset. In fact, I can't stand most spices. I just like to put catsup on my food."*   Well, so much for that person if you enjoy Mexican, Cajun, Thai, Indian, Chinese and all the other spicy foods choices you enjoy. Now you might say to yourself, *"Oh, I don't care if that person doesn't like spicy foods, I can live with that."* Well, can you? If your family likes spicy foods, are you going to call ahead to remind someone to put a pot pie in the oven for your spouse while the rest of your family eats your mom's famous chili? Sitting at the dinner table 365 days a year will have nothing to do with how cute, handsome, tall, short, sexy or any other exterior feature you see when you first meet that person. Not going to a famous restaurant on your anniversary or special occasion because your spouse won't eat the food will indeed chip away at your marriage and don't think for one minute that it won't.

If you want to have children, what would be the point of meeting, dating and marrying someone who has no desire to have children? If you love to ski, why would you want to be with someone that hates the snow? If you want to have a dog or cat, why get involved with someone that hates animals? The point here is very simple. Once you get past the *good looks* of a person, you have to find out what that person is really like. More importantly, you need to focus on your *likes and dislikes* list so you can really know what you are looking for in a relationship. You will be amazed at what happens when you are really aware of the things you like and don't like in life and in another person.

Your list will help you get past the *physical look* and focus on the inner person. It is the inner person that you should marry, not the package he or she came in. Once you know that, you can focus on finding someone with similar likes and dislikes. In this way you will not end up with someone you think you like because of their physical appearance, only to find out later that the real inner person is not someone you like at all.

If you are currently in a unhappy relationship, both of you should make your lists of *likes* and *dislikes*. With that list, you will get a very clear picture of your relationship. Together you will be able to see what the other one is missing in the relationship, which of course is adding to your unhappiness in the relationship, as well as what each of you are doing to *please* the other. You might be surprised at what will happen. After you both address these concerns, there is a good chance that your relationship will move to a new high. On the other hand, you might find that both of you are so *incompatible* that the logical *next step* in the relationship and for both of you is to move on in life separately. If, however, you have invested a lot of time and energy into your relationship, and you can see (from your lists) where the differences are, then professional counseling could be very valuable in helping each of you work out your differences and preserve the relationship.

I remember a great line from a movie years ago called "Love Affair" with Warren Beatty, Annette Bening and the late Katharine Hepburn. Ms. Hepburn asks Annette's character, *"Terry, are you happy?"* She replies, *"I better be, I have everything I ever wanted."* Ms. Hepburn's character replies, *"The trick in life isn't getting what you want, my dear, it's wanting it after you get it."*

The more you know about yourself and what you want out of life, the easier it will be to travel down another one of life's roads. Always give the best of what you have to offer, but don't settle for less in return. Your fate and destiny, when it comes to spending the rest of your life with someone, should be one of happiness, joy, and acceptance with the choice you made in a partner for life. Don't make a lifelong commitment and end up settling for less because of the way someone looks. Keep that list with you at all times and review it often. You're a good person and you deserve to spend the rest of your life with someone that is compatible with you and enjoys the same things you enjoy in life. Now *go for it* and *make it happen!*

A good marriage is like an incredible retirement fund: You put everything you have into it during your productive life, and over the years it turns from silver to gold to platinum.

Willard Scott

*Love one another, but make not a bond
of Love:*

*Let it rather be a moving sea between
the shores of your souls.*

*Fill each other's cup but drink not from
one cup.*

*Give one another of your bread but eat
not from the same loaf.*

*Sing and dance together and be joyous,
but let each one of you be alone,*

*Even as the strings of the lute are alone
though they quiver with the same music.*

*Give your hearts, but not into each
other's keeping.*

*For only the hand of Life can contain
your hearts.*

*And stand together yet not too near
together:*

For the pillars of the temple stand apart,

*And the oak tree and the cypress grow
not in each other's shadow.*

From *The Prophet*
by
Kahlil Gibran

Chapter 18

NEXT—

Love & Marriage

Oh, Love. How wonderful it is! Or is that, how wonderful it was! Is, was, should be? Do you remember *real love?* You know, the goose bumps, hair standing up on the back of your neck. Real love. That's what you called it when you couldn't wait to talk to your *lover*, wasn't it? The candlelight dinners, soft music, those great romantic weekends. Remember that? How about this. "I now pronounce you husband and wife." Remember your wedding day? That day you just knew that you would be so happy for the rest of your life because you married that wonderful person you love. The one that made you so happy and you just knew you would have such a wonderful life together.

Well, are you still just as happy and still that much in *love* as on your wedding day? Does the statement *"going through the motions"* ring a bell?

If you have been married for less than 10 years and you think everything in your marriage is just great -- guess again. The chances of you being just as happy in your marriage today as you were the day you got married is nothing short of a fantasy. Now, before you get all defensive, be truthful with yourself. No one, no couple, no husband and wife, no individual can stay emotionally on top of a feeling of *love* during the long-term relationship of marriage. Now that doesn't mean that you don't love your spouse. Obviously you do or you wouldn't still be together, or would you?

What is important to understand about *next* and marriage is that all couples, no matter how long or short a time they have been married, need to interject a *next step* into their relationship once in a while. I'll bet that if you have been married between five and ten years, you have flashbacks to some of those exciting and passionate times you had before you got married. Maybe you even think of other people you knew before you met your spouse. Someone with whom you may have had a romantic weekend. Remember that person who you sipped champagne with while you fed each other strawberries? That great *goose bump* feeling you had whenever you thought of him or her. You know what I mean. It is not unrealistic for you to fantasize about getting away from that dull day-in-day-out routine that you are now living. For just one night or a short weekend you would love to get your blood flowing again with someone that makes you feel really alive. Someone that cares for you the way your spouse used to do, but somehow doesn't see you that way anymore. Believe me, if you feel that way, you're not alone. Many men and woman get the "seven year itch" when they feel that the magic is gone from the marriage. When that happens it is definitely time to take that *next step* in your relationship.

The following story explains what happened in my marriage and how *next* played such an important part in our relationship. What you're about to read can work for both males and females. This is a perfect example of taking that *next step* in your relationship with your spouse.

My Story: My wife, Mary, and I had been married for about seven years, and if you asked anyone about our marriage, they would have said *"Oh, they are a very happily married couple."* It was a second marriage for both of us. My first marriage lasted less than a year with no children. Mary had four children from a previous marriage of ten years and had moved to California after her divorce. We met at the hospital where we both worked. Her two youngest children (boy and girl) came with her while her two older sons stayed with their dad. The boys would come out to California for half the summer and then all four would go back to spend the second half of summer with their father.

I did all the things that any good father or stepfather would do: PTA meetings, little league, family three-day weekend vacations and the ever so popular two-week vacations (even taking the dog along) with all four of the kids. We did everything from camping to river running to boat cruises. During school I would help with homework, help out at after school activities and just about everything you could do to try and be a good role model parent. Then it happened, and I will never forget it!

One Wednesday night, as I was just about 30 seconds away from falling into a deep sleep, Mary says *"There is something wrong with our marriage."* I opened my eyes and like any good husband said *"Huh?"* She says: *"I said, there is something wrong with our marriage."* I sat up slowly, turned on a light and again said *"Huh?"* Mind you that at this point in my life, I was a happily married man that thought he had a happy marriage. However, for the next hour and half, my wife tried to explain how unhappy I should be and went on to explain how unhappy she was in our marriage and relationship. She expressed her feelings of how she didn't think the marriage could go on unless we were to do something about our relationship. She said that the closeness she once felt for me was gone and if we didn't *"do something"* the marriage could be over. She said that we were both just *going through the motions of a happy marriage*, and something had to change.

By the time we went to sleep, I can assure you of one thing. I was confused. What happened to *my happy marriage?* What did she mean when she said *"the closeness was gone?"* My God, if I got any closer I'd be on her side of the bed. And what did she mean that we had to *"do something?"* What was I supposed to do that I wasn't already doing? What was I missing? Talk about going to sleep perplexed — my head was spinning.

The next morning Mary had already left for work before I got up. That evening at dinner we did not talk about the conversation the night before. When we went to bed she asked if I wanted to talk about it. I told her "No." I still needed a little time to digest all that conversation.

By Friday I just had to talk to someone about this unexpected dilemma. So I called up an old friend of mine, a woman, that I had always enjoyed talking to and being with. I asked her if she could meet me for a drink after work. She said that she would love to meet me and looked forward to seeing me. I will never forget watching her walk into that cocktail lounge at the hotel. Here was a woman that had come straight from work, yet she looked as though she had spent the whole day getting ready to meet with me. She looked fresh, vibrant, and sexy. When I caught her eye she looked excited to see me. She sat down, we ordered a drink and started talking. We talked and we talked and we talked. Wow - it was great! I was having a chance to just sit and engage in a relaxing conversation without the distractions of television, children arguing, dogs barking, telephone ringing and the typical everyday dinner time hustle and activity. The television behind the bar may have been on, but we were not listening or watching it. We were too busy listening to each other.

That was such a great experience and such a change from the life I had been living each night that I asked her if we could meet again next Friday, same place, same time, and she said *yes*. However, that following Tuesday I found out that I had to leave town on business that coming Friday and would not be back until Saturday. When I called to tell her we couldn't meet on Friday, I could tell by the tone in her voice that she was disappointed. I am really not sure what made me ask, but I suggested that she go with me on my business trip. I no sooner suggested it when we both started talking about the fun we could have. Well, she went with me and that was the start of a long term relationship with my lover. Every time I would have to leave town, I would try to take her with me. In fact, we had so much fun together that we would sneak off and check into a hotel just so each of us could have a great experience with the opposite sex.

I am sure that by this point, you are probably thinking a little less of me than when you started this chapter, and I can't blame you. After all, for any guy to step out on his wife is really an S.O.B., to put it mildly. But let me see if I can regain some respect by informing you that my woman, and my lover, is in fact -- my wife. That's right. The woman I met in the cocktail lounge was indeed my wife, Mary.

When I called her up on that Friday, I told her that I needed to talk to her about the conversation on Wednesday night, but that I wanted to talk in a different environment, not at home. And yes, she did look great walking into the place. Most important of all, I had been in this marriage and relationship for over seven years and I was not going to let her walk out of my life because she felt that something was missing in our marriage. If we had a problem, as she saw it, then I wanted to be able to understand what it was and what had to be done in order to fix it. In short, what was the *next step* I had to take to make this marriage continue to work for us?

The long and the short of it can be put into one word. *Communication.* Sure we were going through the motions of being married, but that was the problem according to Mary. They were just the motions of the day-to-day routine and a set pattern of events. We had both fallen victim to the *daily routine* of being married. Mary wanted a marriage that was more than just routine. I honestly had no idea that Mary was unhappy with our relationship. I could very well have become one of those husbands who comes home one day to find a note that says "I have left you...." Mary, however, did take that *next step* and spoke up that Wednesday night, and that changed our fate and destiny forever.

I did take Mary with me when I went on that business trip and it was *GREAT*. For the first time, in a long time, we had a chance to get away from that *daily routine*. It worked out so well that on occasions going forward, we would make arrangements for someone to watch the kids from Saturday at 2 p.m. until Sunday afternoon. Then we would get into the car and drive for a full five minutes -- that's right, five minutes. We would go from our home to a hotel at the airport five minutes away. We would check in, grab a bottle of champagne, run up to our room and put the *do not disturb* sign on the door. At 9 p.m we would get dressed up for the evening and go down stairs to the hotel restaurant and enjoy last wave dining (that's when you are one of the last to be seated for the evening and no other dining customers are coming in). As with all last wave dining, we were able to relax. The food wasn't hurriedly thrown at us. We took our time and ate slowly. Our plates had that little extra bit of food, compliments of the kitchen staff, and we enjoyed our evening of dining in a nice restaurant. As my dad would say, *"We closed the place."*

This also gave us a chance to sleep in late the next morning, leave the hotel and meet friends for a nice Sunday brunch. Arriving back home around 2 p.m., we were refreshed, relaxed, recuperated and our kids barely missed us, if at all. We took these little trips and found time for ourselves until our daughter turned 18 and was off on her own.

The moral to this story is that both of us acted on the situation and took that *next step*. My wife related to me her discomfort in our relationship, a relationship I thought was the way it was supposed to be. By taking action and opening the doors to communication, we were doing something to put our marriage back on the right track. Together we took our relationship to a new and unexpected level and it has stayed way up there ever since.

Mary and I have been married since 1974. Today, with the kids all grown up, living their own lives, *we take the time to find the time* for special moments right in our home and more recently, in our motor home as we travel. We eat dinner every night by candlelight. We stop to watch the sunset. We make sure that no matter how busy we may be that we find the time for each other.

Now that is my story, but let me ask you something. What is your relationship with your partner like right now? Are things just going along status quo or is it time to shake a little spice on that marriage? When was the last time the two of you just took off without the kids and had a little old fashioned fun?

I find it sad when we come across a couple that dated for five years and then split up. In many cases they will tie up with someone else and then five or six years later they leave that relationship. For many, they never find a lifelong relationship. I honestly don't think it is a lack of commitment as much as a lack of communication. Without talking about your feelings *toward each other*, there becomes a lack of feelings *about each other*. The end result becomes an absence of understanding on how to keep the *fire* going in your relationship.

Is it time for you to take that *next step* and put some of that old magic back into your relationship. Why not *go for it* and *make it happen (again)*.

Authors Note: While what I just wrote about happened many years ago, Reba McEntire released a song a while ago titled *Love Needs A Holiday*, and if I didn't know better, I would say it was written for my wife and I. The lyrics mirror what I just wrote. Listen to it when you have a chance.

Chapter 19

NEXT—

Is There a Teenager in the House?

If you are raising children, especially teenagers, you must understand how to take that *next step* and put it to use in your family life. When you think back to your days as a teenager, I am sure you can remember some of the trying times you had growing up. It is extremely important that you realize your teenagers are going through the same hard times. Sure, the influences of today may be different than they were when you were a teenager, but it is all relative to the time in which the teenager is growing up. After all, in the 1950s, they wouldn't even show Elvis Presley below the waist when he first came on television. Today, music videos leave little to the imagination when they display sexual attraction in their videos. If you think you can shelter your teenager from what society has out there, guess again. All you can do is teach your children the difference between right and wrong and how to take the *next step* and move away from a negative situation. This is especially true when peer pressure to do something wrong comes into play. After you teach them the basic rules of right and wrong and that the quickest way for people to lose respect for you is to tell lies (chapter 21), then all you can do is what your parents did -- keep an eye out for telltale signs of trouble. The challenge for an adult/parent is to be able to recognize your child's *telltale behavior* and signs that *something is wrong here.* As much as you may love your children, teenagers realize that it's their life and they are looking for their own identity, not yours. However, if you are going to assume the role of a parent then you need to be one step ahead of every situation with that teenager and remember five simple rules.

1. Be the type of parent you want your children to become, teach by example.

2. Let them know that you love them for who they are, and that your responsibility as a parent is to watch out for their well-being. Help prepare them for life as an adult (irrespective of how they may appear to be turning out).

3. Share your stories of growing up and especially the *mistakes* you made and the consequence you suffered. Also, share the correct choices and good times you had.

   IMPORTANT: Do not glorify or brag about law breaking stunts you may have taken part in. Drag racing, skipping school, hitchhiking, stealing, etc. When you brag about these types of events you are just setting your teenager up to try it also. After all, nothing really happened to you, so why shouldn't they try it.

4. Learn to communicate as a family. Get your kids involved in family conversations.

5. As much as you want to *believe* your teenager would
   only do the right thing and would never lie to you, it
   is sometimes better to *believe* in your *instincts* and *gut
   feelings*. You have every right, as a parent, to check
   out the activities of your teenager whether they like it
   or not. Always follow through on what and where
   they claim to be going.

With teenagers, *next* means opening the lines of
communication. Teenagers of every generation have always
felt that the older they get, the dumber their parents get.
Around the time they grow up and turn 25, they suddenly
discover that their parents seem to get smarter. But what do
you do during that *teenage* period to help both the teens and
the parents stay in touch with each other? You take that *next
step* in every situation you can by talking and opening the
lines of communication between you and them. After all,
teenagers see the situation of growing up as *me verses them*.

You will never be able to get into your teenager's mind.
But you can sure get them to open a few doors to their
thoughts and feelings if you establish a method to do so
before they become a teenager. When you fail to teach your
children how to express their feelings while they are young,
you take away your right to expect that seventeen year old to
suddenly open up and start telling you how they feel. Some
adults still don't know how to express themselves because
they never learned how to do so when they were young.
Don't let your child be one of them. Teach them to
communicate feelings now, before it is too late.

What will work in one household may not work in
another family's setting. Here is something that you can try
that will help open the doors to conversation. It is called the
Sunday newspaper.

The Sunday paper (in print or on the Internet) has
something for everyone in the family, including teenagers.

Just about every teen loves movies and music. Therefore, the calendar section of a Sunday paper is full of new movies, reviews, and a sections on music. Even if your teenager has problems reading, he or she can take all the time they want to look through the calendar section to get ready for the Sunday night newspaper review. That will be the time that everyone in the house sits down at the dinner table and talks about what articles they liked or disagreed with in the Sunday paper.

Between the lifestyle sections, local news page, sports, book review, and front page, everyone in the house finds just one thing to *bring to the table* and talk about during dinner.

Some teenagers may not participate right away. If you have a younger child in the house, encourage them to speak up about the article they read. In time, your teenager will come around and join in too. If they don't, well – maybe they don't care for dessert tonight!

Make it a fun time. Ask for and encourage opposing viewpoints. Explain that no one is to *cut down* anyone's view on an issue. Statements such as *"that's stupid"* or *"your dumb"* do not have a place at the dinner table. Each person gets to give their comments on what they read. Encourage your kids to *get involved* in the discussion. Do this for a full year. Let everyone look at that Sunday paper and select what they want to talk about. If two people select the same thing, that's OK. You might be surprised at their different viewpoints, but most of all (and in time) you will start to see how your teenager thinks.

Once in a while, you can pick the subject and make it an open forum for discussion. Subjects like teenage runaways, suicide, drunk driving, guns, and the one that every parent should talk *openly* about, teenage pregnancy.

These are your children. It is up to you to help them along the road of life. Remember, in chapter 11 I talked about "life is a puzzle." Your teenager also has all the pieces of their puzzle of life right in front of them. Don't you want them to pick up the good and positive pieces? They could be tempted (by others) to go for the more exciting, yet life threatening pieces if you don't help guide them. Right and wrong, good and evil, smart choices, stupid choices— they are right there in front of them. If you think your teenager is having an easy time selecting their pieces of the puzzle, think again. They need your help. Even if they don't come right out and ask you for help, you should know, from your own teenage experience, that they need the correct answers to many of life's problems.

There is probably no better time to help a teenager understand the principles of taking that *next step* in any of life's situations than right now. Explain chapters of this book to them. Help them develop a decision making attitude in life. Talk about morals, responsibility, integrity, and devotion to family. How important it is to be caring, loving, and have compassion for others and life in general.

Make sure you understand the five rules outlined at the front of this chapter, especially number five. That one can make the difference between helping your teenager or becoming a parent that ends up saying *"I can't believe my child would do that."* All parents want to *believe* that their children would not do *"that,"* whatever *that* may be. This is their hope. But you have to draw on your memories as a youth and the things you know other teenagers may have done at that time that were wrong or resulted in disaster. Unless you are going through a life in total denial of everything happening around you, it may be time to stop and really take a good look at your teenager. After all, you raised this child and you know what correct behavior is. If it has changed, go with your gut feeling and investigate.

Don't become a parent who *hopes* nothing is wrong.

Believe your instincts. If you investigate something and your teenager gets upset, explain that you are concerned for his or her well-being and you are doing this out of love and the safety of your child. The very fact that you tell them you are doing this out of _love for them_, in time, it will resonate with them.

One day you will wake up and realize that your teenagers are not teenagers any more, but young adults. You may be hoping that day comes sooner than later, but the day will come. If you want your children to go out into the world with a positive understanding of life and people, believe me, they will not get it from school. It's up to you. Life and teenagers. The ultimate test of _next step_.

True Story: A longtime friend of mine had a daughter that turned 13. One night she was in the alley in back of their house talking with friends and he called her into the house. When she came in he said _"That's it for tonight, I don't want you outside anymore."_ She started complaining saying _"Why? We're not doing anything wrong, we're just talking."_ He started insisting, she kept asking _"Why?"_ and they ended up in a verbal argument with his daughter running off to her room crying. He sat down in a chair for a few minutes and then got up and went into her room. He sat on the edge of her bed and said: _"I guess when you come right down to it, you really were not doing anything bad. You're right in back of the house with your friends, which is better than hanging out on some street corner. Look, you're my oldest daughter and the first teenager in the house. I've never raised a teenager before and this is all new to me."_ She looked up at him and said: _"Gee dad, I've never been a teenager before and this is all new to me too."_

If you live to be 80 or 90 years old, the five years you spent raising a teenager will seem like nothing, yet, at the time it seems like a lifetime.

Jerry X Shea

It is amazing to hear young people who turns about 25 state that they suddenly realize how smart their parents really are.

A statement many parent experiences
once their children are grown.

If money is your hope for independence,
you will never have it. The only real security
that a man can have in this world is a reserve
of knowledge, experience and ability.

Henry Ford (1863-1947)

Chapter 20

NEXT—
The Have And Have
Not Of Money

Do you measure life and your success with a dollar sign? Do you feel that material objects you own or the possessions you have determine how successful you are? Many people do, but unfortunately they do not know or understand the true meaning of a full and happy life.

Just about everyone that you could ask, especially younger people, will most likely say that *more money, winning the lottery, owning bigger and better possessions would make them a happier person.* That is not what the overall picture (puzzle) of life is about.

It is not to say that you wouldn't be happy for a short while if you suddenly became showered with financial wealth. However, after the novelty of moving into the bigger house, filling it with all the expensive *toys*, buying the fancier car and taking the long extended vacation, you would suddenly find that your life really hasn't changed. Your surroundings may have changed, but your family members, friends and everything that made *you* the person *you* are, will still be the same. After all, you were not born into wealth, you just suddenly found yourself in it, and that is not *you.*

How many times have you read in the paper about someone who won a lottery or inherited a lot of money, only to turn up flat broke a few years later? If you get anything out of this book, even if you don't want to take a *next step* in your life, please don't go through life thinking that if you win the lottery you would be a happier person. Free money is not the answer to a happy life.

To dramatize this, let's take a look at a complete stranger on the street. Let's start with a hobo (not to be confused with a homeless person) who has no job, who is all alone, and just passing through your town. He is a fellow human being. Assume that he is male, 6'2" tall, 165 lbs., much like millions of other men. However, if we were to ask him if he was happy with his life, most people would be shocked if he answered "Yes." What if he was indeed happy with life? What if he said he has no money problems, no responsibilities except to himself, and has always found food to eat and a place to sleep? He heads south for the winter and north for the summer. He enjoys all the seasons, and has tasted the different cultural foods that our country has to offer. He enjoys life, meets and talks to great people, and hasn't a care in the world. Believe it or not, there are people like this and there is even a National Hobo Convention held in Britt, Iowa (for over 100 years) on the second weekend in August. If you were that person could you be happy?

Let's look at a middle income person, married, two children, home owner, new car and a nice job. This person is also a fellow human being. Assume she is female, 5' 6" tall, 135 lbs. and from the physical standpoint is also very much like millions of other women. If we were to ask her if she is happy and where she wants to be in life, what do you think she would say? Would she say that she loves the challenges that life brings to her, or would she say life has been hard on her? Being married, raising children, keeping up with the demands of her boss and the job are just too much and she wishes everything would just *go away* so she could just relax? What would you say here?

What about a person that in your eyes *has it made in life?* He has a big house, fancy cars, boat in the marina and a private plane. What do you think this person would say if you asked him if he is happy with his financial status and where he wants to be in life? Would you be amazed if he said he wants *more money?* What would you think if he said he was not where he wanted to be. He wants to be in a bigger house, on a larger piece of property, with a bigger boat, bigger plane and fancier car? On the other hand, what if he said he wishes he could go back to the better days of his life, when he didn't own so much and life seemed easier? Would you be shocked if he said that all his wealth brought him was nothing but a terrible marriage that ended in divorce, he can't see his kids except every other weekend, and life has been full of nothing but problems?

There is nothing wrong with having extra money so you can make your life a little more comfortable. Taking a second job, advancing in your current job, or just working harder to make some extra cash is part of the American lifestyle. That is a great goal in life. To be obsessed with the fantasy that you need to make a lot more money to be happy is another one of America's great tragedies. It results in gambling away hard earned money on the off chance you'll *hit it big*. It results in risks that are far beyond what you should be taking and most important of all, it is almost a guarantee that your relationship with loved ones will be destroyed. Just imagine if you put all that energy into your work and focused on being the very best employee at the company.

Another American weakness is that our society wants financial wealth *now*. People seem to lack the ability and understanding that if you start saving *today* you'll have a nice little "nest egg" saved up for *tomorrow* (the future).

I understood, as a teenager, how important it was to save money to get the things I wanted in life. Thus, by saving my money when I first started working at age 15, I entered high school and had my own car (not my mommy's car) to drive to school. I did the same thing when I went into the Navy and became the *one with the car*. While working at my first job after the Navy I continued to save and on my 25th Birthday I drove a new Jaguar XKE off the dealer's lot. While having a *hot car* may be a thing young guys want, it was around that time that a neighbor of my parents, Al Baker, gave me the best savings advice I ever received. He said to me *"Jerry, you need to learn and understand long term savings. I know you do a good job of saving for short term things like your new car, but there are going to be many things in life, other than cars, that you are going to want to purchase and you are going to need a well-designed savings plan to save for it. That even includes your retirement at 65."* With that statement, my mouth just dropped open and I said, *"Al, I'm twenty five years old for crying out loud and retirement is forty years away. You got to be kidding me to think I should start saving for retirement now."* He smiled and said, *"Just because it is a long way off is no excuse to not start some kind of a long range retirement plan now."* Then he said something that really got my attention. *"Jerry, I want to explain to you the principle of 'pay yourself first, and live off the rest.'* He went on to say, *'you need to develop a lifestyle of taking each and every pay check you ever get and before you pay any bills or spend any money, pay yourself first. Put 5%, 10%, 15% of that paycheck, whatever you feel you can comfortably put away, into a mutual fund long term account. If you do it right, then as much as retirement seems a long way off, when that time comes you will be set for the rest of your life. "*

I trusted and liked what Al was telling me and I agreed to open my first IDX mutual fund savings account. I opened it with retirement as the long range goal. Sure I was good at saving money, but other than saving for a car, I really did not have a long range plan and I really liked the idea of putting a set amount away with each paycheck. I decided I would save 15% out of every paycheck I would receive. Even working the other jobs I had, I would take 15% right off the top and put it in a saving account and then at the end of three months transfer the funds over to my mutual fund account. Three years later, and because I had learned to *pay myself first*, I purchased my first home while I was still single.

When I was thirty three years old my employer called an assembly for everyone to attend. It was a short presentation on a new savings program for retirement called a 401K. Simply put, you could take the amount of money you would make in a pay period and put up to 15% into a 401K savings plan (that the employer had set up) and you would then be taxed on what was left, not taxed on your total income. This to me was the ultimate *pay yourself first.*

After the assembly about 12 of us went down to the cafeteria. Sitting around the table I told everyone how great I thought this new savings plan was and that I was signing up right now. You should have seen what happened? Everyone was laughing so hard that some of them where crying. I heard, *"you got to be kidding – you won't retire for over 30 years and you are going to start saving now – what an idiot."*

Of course I was already saving, but it was from my paycheck (pay yourself first) and that was after tax money. This would be pre-tax money. That would mean that when I received my paycheck I would already have *paid myself first* and could now *live off the rest.*

In the early '80s when Individual Retirement Accounts (IRAs) came along, both my wife and I saved money each year to put into an IRA (which also lowered our income and tax base). The goal was to continue to keep putting money into a retirement account for our future. I thought that everyone, by the time they reached their 40s would be saving for retirement. I recently attended my high school reunion and was amazed to find that so many of my fellow classmates had never saved anything for retirement. They are now faced with the reality that while some of us are retired (from the work force), they will have to continue working - forever.

What is amazing about saving money is how so many people think that small amounts ($5, $10, $20 or more a week) put into a savings account, on a regular basis and later transferred to broad based index funds, is just not enough to make a difference in their lives. Yet, if you walked up to someone who never saved for retirement and asked if he or she could use any extra money in retirement do you think anyone would say "no"? What many people fail to understand is just how important saving for the future should be. Social Security will not provide enough money for anyone to live the lifestyle they would like to have. Contact your Social Security office now and find out what your SS check is projected to be when you hit retirement. You will most likely be shocked when you see the monthly amount you will have to try and live off of for the rest of your life if all you have is Social Security. Only some form of a retirement savings plan/account will provide you with the additional money you are going to need to enjoy retirement.

And how can anyone talk about savings without talking about the folks that blow their money on lotto tickets. Did you ever do the math on just how much money over a 30 or 40 year period you will have blown by buying lotto tickets? Yes, I know, *someone has to be the winner.* Well guess what, it is not you. Go ahead, take the amount you spend each week, multiply it by 52 (weeks in a year) and them multiply that by 30 or 40 (years). Just look at that number. Now think of how much more comfortable your lifestyle could be if you had all that money you blew on lotto tickets available, with interest, on the day you retire. If you are a smoker just take the cost of a carton of cigarettes and pencil that one out. That same money invested in a broad based index fund over a 40 year period could give you over $250,000 at retirement. Stop smoking and you can live to enjoy it.

What you will find (today and in the future) when it comes to retirees and a comfortable lifestyle is that there are the "haves" and the "have nots." The haves spent their working years saving for their retirement. The have nots have been buying lotto tickets thinking they will win their retirement. Mark my word. The sad part of retirement is that more people are in the have not group. What group will you be in at retirement?

Regardless of your age today, anytime is a great time to start saving for your future. If you are really young and would like to have that dream car, or own your own home before you're 30, you can do it if you just learn to *"pay yourself first and live off the rest."* Go ahead and take that *next step* towards financial security and the items you would like to have. It's real easy when you set money saving goals to *go for it* and *make it happen.*

SOME OF THE THINGS WE DID AND WHAT YOU CAN ALSO DO TO SAVE MONEY FOR RETIREMENT

• Purchased a Sony Trinitron TV in 1976. Kept that TV until it gave out in 2002. While others purchased the *big black box* large screen TVs in the '80s & '90s, we kept watching our Sony.

- Drove our cars for 8-10 years. While others bought a new car every couple of years we drove ours to over 150,000 miles.

- Wait 6 months until a movie comes out on video/DVD and then pop a bag of popcorn and watch the movie at home.

- We have a place in our house called the *kitchen*. It was designed to cook food in and that is what we do in it seven days a week. Eating out is a waste of your money. Save eating out for birthdays, anniversaries and after the little league game. Want to see where your money goes? Start adding up the receipts from eating out. Learn to cook.

- We would buy a $1 lotto ticket on New Year's Day. Then for the next 52 weeks we put money in the bank and bought an IRA at the end of the year.

- Live within a budget. When you get your paycheck, *pay yourself first and live off the rest.* Put down on paper how much money you have in that pay period. Determine what will be used to pay bills, credit cards, car payments and house payment. What is left is what you have to spend for food and fun. Don't buy anything on a credit card. Spend what you have and when it is gone, that's it until next payday.

- When you shop, price compare. Don't buy food in a *designer grocery store.* Buy the whole chicken, not the cut up pieces. Buy a brick of cheese not cheese slices. Never buy pre-packaged dinners (unless you live alone). Buy a jar of marinade and marinate your own food. Don't buy pre-marinated foods from the deli counter. Become a wise shopper.

It is hard to believe that there are so many simple steps you can take to save for retirement. Just stop wasting your money on things you really don't need today and get by with what you have. Learn to save for the future.

Here are a few more tips:

Spending $20 a week for lotto tickets, over a 30 year period and you will have spent $31,2000.00 dollars. *Stop it.*

Who says you can't have money at retirement? The key is to stop blowing your money on things you really don't need today, and just start saving for the future.

When you see retired people driving around in fancy cars, sitting in nice restaurants, going on cruise ships and staying at vacation resorts, those are the people that saved for retirement.

Compare that with the older couple driving a 20 year old car that walk into a liquor store and buy lotto tickets, a six pack of beer and a pack of cigarettes -- I think you get it.

Start saving today and *make it happen* for your retirement.

Tell the truth and run --- Yugoslavian proverb

Chapter 21

NEXT—

The "Little White Lie"

If you don't tell the truth and you live a life of lies, then eventually you will get *caught in the lie*. When that happens, you end up spending your time trying to justify the lie. This can result in your telling even more lies just to cover up the original lie. Then you have some folks who just have a hard time telling the truth. In an effort to be accepted by others, they end up telling lies so they will be perceived as a different person from who they really are. In some cases, they justify their lie by rationalizing that it was only a *"little white lie and no one got hurt."* Their thinking is, *"telling a lie will make me look smarter, more knowledgeable or acceptable to the group."* Then you have the person who tells a lie because he won't tell the truth and face the consequences. That always seems to be a good excuse for telling that *little while lie.* When we talk about fate and destiny, telling lies is a sure way to guarantee disaster for your future. Even the *little white lie* can make your life miserable.

One of the best examples of telling a lie came from the President of the United States in 1998. That was when President Bill Clinton was caught in one of the biggest and oldest lies in the world. He stood in front of the television cameras and told the American public, *"I did not have a sexual relationship with that woman, Ms. Lewinsky."* That lie, compounded by other lies, almost cost him his presidency. When he finally went back onto television and admitted that he did have a relationship with Ms. Lewinsky, he lost a great deal of credibility and respect in many communities. Worse than that, his lies reconfirmed, in the minds of many, that all politicians are liars. This writer does not believe that because a few people choose to lie, that everyone in that arena is a liar. However, because so many in politics have been prosecuted for lying, embezzlement or taking a bribe, it puts a negative tone on the profession that *they must all be liars.*

The fundamental liar

Although we are talking about the *little white lie*, let's just touch on the *fundamental* liar for just a second. Unfortunately, this person goes through life living a life of nothing but lies. Usually this is a person who is just really looking for acceptance in everything he or she will do and can't handle telling the truth because of the fear of rejection. They lie so much that at times even they can't tell reality from the lie. As the saying goes, *"They live the lie."* These people need professional help. Unless they seek some form of help, they will ultimately destroy themselves. People will classify them as liars and realize in time that they lie to make themselves look good. Do you want to be classified as a *liar?* If not, then don't lie. If you do lie, you will lose the respect of those around you and in time your lies will definitely affect your fate and destiny.

Lying about someone's persona is bad enough. Lying in the workplace when the lie affects other people and a business is a whole new story. When you don't *call it like it is* and stand up to the truth, everyone can get hurt and it could destroy a company, cost you your job or both.

There is no such thing as *a little white lie* in the workplace. To say anything other than the truth, as you know it, is more than lying. It is deceiving, cheating, nonproductive and most important of all, devastating to a department, division or the business as a whole. Everyone at one time or another has come across an individual or even a whole company that has a reputation for *lying* just to get ahead in business. In most cases the companies are short lived. When you make it a practice of lying all the time, you get caught in the lie more times than you think. You can't fool the public at large. When enough people catch on to your lying, you are suddenly the topic of conversation at every gathering. All it takes is for one person to express his or her *bad experience* with you because you lied. All of a sudden everyone is joining in and relating their *bad experiences* with you or your company. Those listening to the open conversation just might have been a prospective customer. Instead they hear how you *lied* about delivering on time, about an item in stock, the final price, or any other *lie*. The prospective customers will be asking people, *"Who else can you recommend?"* People will relate positive experiences when the person or company *did not lie*. If, however, you are from the company known for lying they will certainly not recommend you.

The *"How do I look?"* white lie

The classic example of the *little white lie* is the *"how do I look?"* asked by a spouse who gets a new haircut, buys new clothes, or does anything that changes her every day appearance. When you *look*, if you like what you see you will obviously tell the truth. If you *look*, however, and personally don't like what you see, what are you going to say? If you're a married man and you intend on spending the night in bed with your spouse, what are you going to tell her about that new hairstyle? She just spent half the day in the beauty shop, and, in your opinion her hair looks like she was given an electric shock by mistake. Let's face it, most men do not want to have to put up with the aftermath of telling the truth if, *in their opinion*, they don't like what they see. In many cases, telling the truth will definitely put their marriage to the test.

If you're a wife and your husband just came through the door with a haircut that, in *your opinion*, makes him look like a 50 year old trying to look 20 again, what *in your opinion* are you going to say? What if he walks in the door with a new striped sport jacket that reminded you of a cigar smoking used car salesmen? What would you say?

If you are a husband and your wife puts on the new dress and shoes she just purchased, and in *your opinion*, the dress looks like the sack that potatoes come in and the shoes make her feet look like a size 18, do you give *your opinion* or tell the *"little white lie?"*

Let's break it down a bit. When it comes to telling a spouse the truth about how he or she looks, let's face it, your fate and destiny are really sitting on the fence with whatever answer you give. But again, the best answer is the truth, not a *little white lie*.

So what do you say, if, in *your opinion*, you don't like what they just bought? You say, "I want to be honest and tell you the truth, and in <u>*my opinion*</u>, I don't like it."

You have just told the truth. It may not be what he or she wants to hear, but make sure that they know it is just *your opinion*. You can always say that you don't like the color, style, cut, buttons, or whatever you want to say, if it is telling the truth.

It could just be that your spouse thinks your taste in clothing stinks. In which case he or she will discount your opinion and go on about his or her business. Then again, one of you may be sleeping on the couch tonight.

When it comes to personal expression through clothing, hair, and makeup, most people establish their tastes and habits early in life and carry them through the years, making changes that usually reflect the changing times and age.

We all learn early in life what *colors* work best when we wear them. Once we lock into a style of clothing we feel comfortable in, we usually stick with it.

If a person spends six hours shopping for a new outfit to wear to a special function such as a job interview, meet someone for the first time, or even if it's just clothing to wear to work, if, in *your opinion* that person does not look good in that new outfit, are you going to tell the truth or tell the *little white lie,* "you look great"?

When it comes to someone changing their appearance and asking you *"what do you think,"* the *little white lie* can come back and bite you in the butt if you are not careful and this is how.

First of all, the person is really asking for your acceptance in their decision to change their hair, clothing or make up. If that person didn't care what you thought, he or she wouldn't ask you in the first place. The person would make changes and go about his or her business. Unless of course that person is the type that needs reassurance and acceptance for their change. Many time if you do not notice, then you end up getting a *"You didn't notice"* statement a little later. With human nature being what it is, however, we want to be accepted when we make changes. We look for that acceptance by asking those close to us *"How do I look?"* We want your acceptance so you can reinforce our decision.

And let's face it, all of us at one time or another got a little adventurous when it came to making a change in our appearance. We *tried something new* and then asked someone for acceptance by saying *"How do I look?"*

Now here is where *next* really comes into play. If, in *your opinion*, the new haircut, clothing or makeup doesn't look good on that person, *tell them the truth* by saying to them *"in my opinion, I don't like it because ......"* and give the reason you don't like it. If you feel it makes the person look fat, out of proportion or character, cheap or even unflattering, whatever your reason, tell the truth. If you lie, for fear that you would hurt the person, that lie can backfire on you in a big way.

Now, let's just say that you told a lie and said *"Wow, that looks great."* Because you told that lie, the person goes off to work, to the party, the job interview, or to see a friend with their changed appearance. When he or she comes back they may be all upset because *someone else* told them the truth. The bottom line here is the fact that you told them they looked *great*. Now they realizes that they do not look good dressed that way and realizes, too, that *you lied to them.* How do you think that affects your credibility?

If a complete stranger came up to you and said *"Tell me the truth, what do you think of this outfit?"* Would you lie or tell the truth? Most people would tell the truth. After all, if the person asking the question doesn't like your truthful answer, so what. They asked for your opinion, you gave it and you have nothing to lose by telling the truth. However, when it's your spouse, best friend or co-worker, telling the truth could affect your relationship with that person, right? The problem in not telling the truth, especially if later on that person realizes that you were not truthful, affects your trustworthiness. As a result of a lie your spouse, friend or co-worker may not ask for our opinion in the future.

Obviously, you may run into a situation in which an out and out lie may be the only way to save a life or keep some kind of tragedy from happening. Case in point would be if a crazed gunmen was looking for a person and you had to lie to keep him from killing someone. You can justify that lie.

The bottom line to this chapter is very simple. When asked a question, for an opinion, or for a comment that requires a truthful answer, *tell the truth*. In the long run it will have been the right decision.

Caught In A Lie

I could not complete this chapter without writing about one of the more up-to-date lies that has happened (as I was reviewing the printed proof of this book). This lie really begs the question, *"What made him think he could lie his way out of this?"* Talk about a great example of *IT'S A GREAT LIFE IF YOU DON'T WEAKEN.*

In January 2013, Lance Armstrong admitted to Oprah Winfrey that for all seven of his wins in the Tour de France cycling event, he had indeed "doped" in order to win the events. For years he went on television denying any wrong doing. He put lies on top of lies. Making accusations against others around him and even suing people for inferring that he was doping. He was stripped of all seven wins, lost sponsorships, the respect of the American people and the whole world.

Coming together is a beginning; keeping together is progress; working together is success.

HENRY FORD (1853-1947)

Chapter 22

NEXT—
People of Power

What comes to mind when people say *"He is such a powerful person."* or *"She is in a powerful position?"* We know they are not talking about physical strength. But what do they mean when they say that a person is *powerful?* More importantly, are you intimidated by people at work or play that are perceived as being *powerful?*

When we talk about a *powerful person*, we really need to make sure we are talking about a person with *powerful abilities* in the workplace or community; a person that has the power to get things accomplished, not someone that uses his or her power (position) to demean or control others.

There is an old military saying that *"Everyone puts their pants on one leg at a time."* That simply means that we all do basic things in life the same way. No matter how rich or poor you may be, when it comes to basic functions, we are all the same.

As we grow up, however, we start hearing things such as *'The one with the most gold rules," "The keeper of the keys controls all,"* and *"Rule one, the boss is always right. Rule two, refer to rule one."* These-in-your face, get-in-line, do what you're told statements that young people often hear can cause them to become intimidated by perceived *powerful* persons. Even worse, some learn to use intimidation instead of knowledge when they themselves grow up.

The concept of *next,* as it pertains to dealing with *powerful people*, is for you to recognize that there are individuals that have worked very hard to get to their place in society or at work. One should respect and acknowledge their accomplishments and positions. The genuine people of power understand that they *get dressed each morning one leg at a time* and realize that respect goes in two directions.

Unfortunately, there are people that abuse their position of power and display an attitude of being *"better than you."* Some even misuse their positions by demeaning those under them. They *push* their power onto people and display a *do as I say or I will crush your carrier* attitude.

"Use it, don't abuse it" might apply to power tools, but it is also a great slogan for people in power. Truly powerful people do not abuse their power. They have acquired a level of knowledge and expertise in what they do in the work force or in society. There is great value in that knowledge and many will share their expertise with others by writing a book about their success. Generally, powerful people know the right people to contact to get things done. Their networking abilities and contacts can make a job go more smoothly. They can get answers to questions and help put *the light at the end of the tunnel*. With the knowledge of having been there before in similar situations, the truly powerful person knows how to draw on that knowledge to see that the job gets done and the wheels of progress keep turning.

The person who uses a *position of power* to intimidate others finds it very lonely at the top, that's if such a person even gets to the top. The statement, *"The people you step on as you go up the ladder of success will be the same people you'll meet on your way down."* has held true for many managers that used intimidation as their tool to motivate employees.

The following are two examples of *powerful people* and the sharp contrast between the two.

The Correct Use Of Power

After joining the U.S. Navy at 18, my first assignment was in Meridian, Mississippi, with a flight training squadron. Already having photographic skills, I was assigned to work in the base photo lab while I waited to attend the Navy Photography School in Pensacola, Florida in six months. One of my very first assignments was to take a picture of the captain of the base, at a captains' mast, giving an award to one of the enlisted men who pulled someone from a burning car.

As a new sailor fresh out of boot camp, finding myself going before this *big* captain of the Navy base was a little intimidating to say the least. By thinking *next,* I drew on the fact that the captain put his pants on the same way I did each morning; *one leg at a time.* His position, as the captain of the base, was to present an award to someone in front of a gathering of people. My job, as I got dressed that morning, was to *capture* that moment on film. I attended the ceremony to do my job. The captain was going to the event to do his job.

After some speeches, the moment came. The captain asked the enlisted man to come up and stand next to him as he read the inscription on a plaque. At that moment, I came from the side of the room and walked right up in front of the two of them. As the captain handed him the plaque and shook his hand I took a picture. Then I said; *"Could you hold that pose and look at the camera please?"* and I took a second picture, lowered my camera to see the captain staring right at me with an expression of *surprise.* I turned and walked back over to the side.

When the negatives where developed, I made a print of each and, as ordered, sent them to the captain for him to select the one he wanted to send out with the press release to the newspapers.

One of the other photographer mates in the photo lab saw the prints and said *"hey Shea, where the heck did you stand to get that picture?"* I told him how I got the shot and his face went blank. *"You stood a few feet from the captain? What are you crazy, we never stand that close. We always take the picture from the back of the room. You're an idiot."*

That afternoon a call came into the photo lab and I was told to report to the captain's office immediately. If you think you would get butterflies over just taking the pictures, imagine what it felt like in my stomach when I was told to *"Report to the captain!"* Now, all of a sudden everyone in the photo lab jumped on my case. *"Shea, you are going to the brig – no one has ever been called down to the captain's office." "You jerk, you stood too close." "Oh, man, you are in deep s--- Shea. Looks like your time in the Navy is over."*

On the way to the captain's office, my mind started coming up with all kinds of thoughts. If none of the previous photographers in the photo lab had taken a picture that close to the captain before, what kind of trouble did I get myself into? All of a sudden I saw myself at some court martial because I stood too close to the captain, or I disrupted the ceremony, or who knows what? Why would the captain want to see me? What did I do? What should I have done differently?

When I arrived at the captain's office the yeoman told me to sit down until I was directed to go in. *GO IN* --- AAHHHHHHHH - Would I ever *"Get out?"*

Then all of a sudden **"Shea, the captain will see you now!"** Gulp! I got up, opened the door, walked up to the captain's desk, saluted him and stood at attention. He said, *"At ease, Shea, take a seat."* He picked up the pictures, looked me in the eye and said, *"I have been in command of this new base since it opened six months ago, and this is the best photograph ever taken at a captain mast, and the best picture of me. All these other photographers take the photo from the back of the room and they don't come out very sharp. These are great."* Suddenly feeling a sigh of relief I said *"Thank you, sir."* He then asked me when I had graduated from the Navy photography school. I explained that I was waiting to *attend* in six months. He asked me about my photographic experience and how I learned to take pictures. I explained that I got interested in photography when I was 12, took photo/art classes in school and was the school's photographer for the newspaper and annual. Then he said; *"Who do you report to in the photo lab and what is the name of the officer in charge of your division?"* I gave him their names and he said, *"From now on, I want you to be my personal photographer at the events I attend. I also want you to be the photographer for the officers' wives luncheon that my wife puts on once a month. Their pictures have not been very good either."*

Now, there is no doubt that the captain of the base has a very responsible and powerful position. But he was human, approachable, and wanted nothing more than the respect that his position demanded, including some decent photos of the events on base. From that point forward and for the next 24 months, I was the captain's official photographer. He spoke to me, not at me, and respected my place in doing my job and getting the best pictures possible. If for some reason a flash bulb (remember this is back in the early '60s) didn't go off, he would wait until I put in a new one and took the picture. When an admiral would come to the base, he would introduce me to him and tell him that I would be following them around taking pictures. The officers' wives monthly luncheons were great. Lots of good food and nothing but women (all married to officers, of course). That one incident, of taking a picture the correct way, and not being intimidated by someone's position, changed my fate and destiny while I was stationed in Mississippi. In fact, I put in a request not to attend photography school and just studied the book and took the test. I passed the test the first time I took it and became an official Navy photographer, 3rd class.

Now, in sharp contrast, some twenty years later while working for a large company, I had another very memorable experience.

The Wrong Use Of Power

The company had hired a new president. He was young and the classic example of someone who abuses his power by intimidating everyone around him.

One could respect his ability to get to the position of president, especially considering that he went back to school to advance his career. But somewhere, somehow, he picked up *intimidation* as a means of management. Employees in supervisory and vice president positions started leaving within months after he came on board. One vice president that had been with the company for years, held many key positions, was a good leader of people, stopped me one day to say that he was leaving the company because of the new president. During the Korean War that vice president was an ace fighter pilot and he said *"I don't need to put up with his type of intimidation and demeaning behavior. Life is too short and I am not going to work for this jerk."* (Actually, he used another word for "jerk").

I reported to a VP who reported directly to this president. This meant that, at times, we both would meet with him. In his office he had moved his desk and chair on a platform eight inches above the rest of the floor and placed a couch in front of his desk that when you sat in it, you sank real low. This gave him that _looking down at you_ perspective, emphasizing his superiority, while you had to _look up_ to him, as servants, from your lower positions. This was classic textbook _"management by intimidation."_

This president always called meetings and would have 15 to 20 people in a room, to review a plan or project. Then he would give his standard line _"I want a full written report from each of you with your viewpoints on this tomorrow morning."_ No matter what it was, everyone was always busy writing reports for this man. He had supervisors writing reports, directors writing reports and vice presidents writing reports. One department supervisor was trying to finish five reports from meetings he had attended the day before. This president had so many people writing reports that went to just him, not a group or a committee, that it would be impossible for one person to read them all.

There was only one way we could do anything and that was his way. Whatever it was, he had to put in his two-cents and make changes. Upper management developed a real dislike for this guy; while lower management and some employees feared him.

The day came when he was offered a job in another state (or maybe told to go find another job?). On his last day, the company gave him a going-away party. Everyone turned out to say goodbye. Some out of fear, most out of joy! Everyone, that is, but me.

This person had power, but abused it. People could not respect him because he did not respect them as individuals. He was now leaving. Everyone was pleased. I had dealt with him as best I could on a business to business level, but that is where it stopped.

At 4:45 p.m. on his last day of his employment with the

company and knowing that I did not attend his going away party, he had his secretary call my office and ask that I come up and see him. After I received the message, I paused for a second and collected my thoughts. There was no official business left to talk about, so why would he want to see me? It was no secret that I had voiced my displeasure at his management style. Now, 15 minutes before the end of the day and the end of his job there was no way that I was going to give him the opportunity of place me in his *low slung chair* again while he stood up on his *high perched platform* and read me the riot act. I knew he wanted to take a *parting shot.* I waited a few minutes and called his secretary back. She said *"Mr. Shea, he is waiting for you."* I said to her, *"Look, your job as his secretary is to make sure he gets all his messages, right?"* She said, *"Yes – but are you coming up?"* I said *"No."* There was a moment of silence. Then in a very concerned and low slow voice she said *"Ooohhh Jerry—I don't know if that's a good idea."* I told her not to worry about me, to just do her job and to relate to him that I would not be coming to his office.

When I hung up the phone, I put on my coat and locked my office door. As I left I told another director, still in her office, that I felt that the president might be coming down to look for me. I told her to just tell him I was gone for the day. She replied *"Oh Jerry, are you sure you know what you are doing?"*

I went straight to my car and headed for home. Within two minutes after I left, sure enough, the president came *running* down the steps to my office and banged on the door for me to open it. He turned to the director and barked *"Where is he?"* She told him I had gone home for the day. With that, he turned and bolted back up the stairs and went directly to the personnel office. He stormed right into the office of the head of personnel, told him to pull my employee file and demanded that I be terminated right then and there.

News of this happening spread like wild fire throughout the whole organization. When I arrived at work on Monday morning, the employees at the front lobby started clapping their hands as I walked in. On the way to my office, managers and department heads stepped out from all over the place and started shaking my hand and thanking me for standing up to a person that had *looked down on them.* The head of the personnel department called me into his office and told me about the president's request for my termination. We both sat there and enjoyed a good laugh. By lunchtime the whole building knew what had happened and when I walked into the cafeteria I got a standing ovation. His secretary, a 20 year employee, came over to me and confessed that working for him had been the worst years of her employment. She said she had never typed so many meaningless reports in her life. She, too, was intimidated by his actions and feared for her job.

The contrast between my experience with the captain of the Navy base and this president was as great as night and day. People with power and authority that respect those in other positions are the genuine people of power. The ones that try to intimidate others by abusing their power do not have true power. It is a misconceived power.

Books and people that try to teach others to *"win by intimidation"* are doing a great disservice to humanity and the business world. Getting ahead by *intimidation* is not getting ahead at all. It destroys relationships. Eventually, intimidators find they don't really have any power at all. They only have the ability to *turn people off.* After all, one of your greatest powers is your ability as an individual to say *next* and take control of your own life. You should not be intimidated by anyone.

If you are a person of power, or you are working up to a

position of authority, make it a daily practice to respect those around you. After all, if something adverse happens to you on your way up the ladder of success, such as a cut back or a corporate merger, you will want all the people you meet on the way down to be your allies. If you stepped on them on your way up, your bad reputation will follow you wherever you go, stifling your ability to find another job. Make it your personal motto to respect everyone you meet. Never impose respect. Now, *go for it* and *make it happen..*

Chapter 23

NEXT—

Business and Sales

Without a doubt, understanding *next* and knowing how and when to take that *next step* is an absolute must in business, especially for the small business owner. A business owner has to make quick decisions and learn how not to get *stuck on hold* with situations that can't be changed. He must know how to put out the many *fires* that pop up in business (issues with employees, vendor and customers.). Basically small business owners have to learn how to *next* the many daily situations that are constantly coming at them. They must also do their best to keep their company moving forward. The inability to constantly take that *next step* and adjust to changes in your industry and your business will be a sure sign of failure for that business.

One of my most memorable examples of *next* took place on February 15, 1994, when Viacom beat out QVC for the takeover of Paramount Pictures in what the Los Angeles Times called *"the biggest takeover war of the 1990s."* Barry Diller, Chairman of QVC, who had lost the bid, said *"They won. We lost. Next."* Even though this takeover war went on for many months, it was over. To sit around and mope about it would be a waste of time and energy. Mr. Diller

204   IT'S A GREAT LIFE IF YOU DON'T WEAKEN

commented on exactly what he had to do now that he lost his bid for the takeover. Just move on down the line and see what's *next*. I remembered hearing his statement on a radio news broadcast while driving home and my mouth just dropped open. Here was someone with the power of millions of dollars behind him and he says *"next,"* moving on in both business and in life. Obviously, Mr. Diller does not have to read this book. He is already using *next* in his life. Most likely, that philosophy is what got him to his position in the first place.

If you are a successful business owner, you most likely already exercise some form of *next* in your everyday activities. If you are thinking of going into business, answer *"yes"* or *"no"* to the following questions: Do you know how to make quick decisions? Can you move through a number of projects at one time? Could you handle three customers at the same time if they all came to you with complaints? Do you know if you could handle disgruntled employees? If you answered *no* to these few questions, do everyone a big favor --- don't go into business.

The ability to operate a small business and wear the hats of everything from President to the weekend janitor requires skills that some people just don't have and will never develop. As the owner of a business, you are not only trying to make an income for yourself, you also bear the responsibility of income to all of your employees. Vendors will also be relying on your success to help keep them in business. Spending too much time on one area of your business (because you can't take that *next step* in a situation) could result in a total breakdown of your compete business.

Of course, the number one priority of any business is creating *sales*. If you talk to any seasoned sales professional, he or she will tell you that *next* is the key word in all sales attempts. When the salesperson cannot get to the buyer, decision maker or purchasing agent to purchase what you are trying to sell to them, then all you can do for that moment is say to yourself *next* and move on quickly to your next prospective buyer. The ratio of rejection is the highest for salespeople who learn very quickly to *next* every *"no"* they receive. The slogan for many salespeople that make sales calls by phone is *"smile and dial"* and that is what they do all day long. Can you?

Rejection didn't stop Mark Victor Hansen and Jack Canfield who were turned down by over 32 publishers when they tried to find one to publish their first *Chicken Soup for the Soul* book. At one of their seminars, Mark was using an overhead projector to show statements and cartoons while he spoke. He said "When you talk to a publishing house, if they say *'NO'* you say *'NEXT'* and just keep trying." He then put up a color image of the word *NEXT*. The big crashing sound from the side of the room was me falling off my chair. Here these New York Times best-selling authors confirmed my very belief and way of life. Keep moving forward and *next* the situation.

In his talk and book <u>Dare to Win,</u> Mark relates his tough times in life when he was twenty-six years old and hit bottom. A friend told him he *"had to succeed."* It is very obvious that Mark Victor Hansen was not the type of person to sit there and let obstacles stop him from moving forward in life. On May 25, 1999, three versions of their *Chicken Soup for the Soul* had the first, second and third positions on the New York Times best seller list. Imagine being an author with not one, not two, but three best sellers all at one time in the same week. Do you think these guys take *next* seriously?

In my book <u>*IT LOOKS EASY! IS IT? Simple Steps for Small Business Success,*</u> the topics of sales, advertising, pricing, employees, and all the aspects of a business are discussed with an emphasis on the importance of *next*.

In the world of business, big or small, one has to develop a way to keep moving forward and not get stuck on hold. A person's ability to continuously upgrade his knowledge of their industry plays an important part in his success. Constantly applying *next* to your way of thinking and to the actions you take is what will put you on the road to success. Knowing how to *next* each and every situation will prove to be far more important than your knowledge of a particular field. Nothing works better than taking that *next step,* a decision to *go for it* and putting in the effort to *make it happen.*

If you are thinking of going into business for yourself, you may want to read my two business books;

It Looks Easy! Is It? Simple Steps for Small Business Success. This book explains what the daily life of a small business owner is really like. If you have never owned your own business, you may be surprised at what you read.

Prospecting – Presentation – Close, Your Three Keys To Successful Sales. You cannot close the sale unless you have made some form of a presentation. However, you can't make that presentation unless you are in front of a prospective buyer. Learn all three and your sales success is just around the corner.

Chapter 24

NEXT—

What Do You See
When You See?

If you understand how your fate and destiny can be changed by using *next,* then we have but one final point to discuss in order to come full circle in this book. Let me ask you an important question: *"What do you see, when you see?"*

I am not taking about your ability to see with your eyes in order to describe something. I'm talking about your ability to interpret situations that come before you in your personal life, the lives of those around you, and your work.

In the Merriam-Webster Collegiate Dictionary some of the definitions of the verb *see* is; *"to come to know: to form a mental picture of: visualize – to imagine as a possibility."* Do we really have to physically *see* something in order to *see*? Can you imagine how great your life could be if all you ever let your mind *see* is the good positive things that life has to offer? Think about it. Instead of seeing everything around you as being old, worn out or used, you *next* it and are glad that you at least have possessions that others may not ever have. Instead of seeing the wrong in someone, look for the good in that person.

If you find yourself stuck in traffic, you *next* it and take that time to listen to your favorite music. Listen to the recording of a lecture or a book on tape. Learn to use this *stuck in traffic* time as positive time. If you think your life has problems, just tune into a talk radio program and listen to all the people calling in with their problems. Problems that make your problem seem like a drop in the bucket.

Take a second right now to look around you. How do you *see*, what you *see*? Do you see good, positive things?

At this point you should have an understanding of how *next* and taking that *next step* can work for you. Do you have the enthusiasm to look at life with more of a positive attitude about yourself and life in general? If you have read this whole book, then you are ready to *go for it?*

You can put it to the test right now. The very next person you meet (family member, friend, neighbor, co-worker, boss, whoever it is) just *stop* what you are doing and talk to them. Make a favorable comment about what they are wearing. Ask them about their weekend, their family, dog, car, anything you want. The idea is to engage in conversation. Step out of the *me* box and step into the box of *life.*

Changing your fate and destiny is so easy you'll actually amaze yourself when you do it. The first and most important key in making a change in your fate will be a conscious decision to take that *next step.* Once you make the commitment to change your fate and destiny, then all you have to do in order to start the changing process is to be *happy.* That's right, believe it or not, happiness is a major *next step* in creating a change in your life's direction. That happiness will have a profound effect on your fate and destiny. Once you make the conscious decision to brighten up your life by being a happier person, astonishing changes will occur and change you.

Here is a very simple question for you: If you keep going the way you are now going will the next five years of life be a carbon copy of your last five? Are you ready to take that *next step* out of the dark and gloom of your carbon copy days and step into the sunlight of an exciting life? No one can take that first step for you. Each first step really starts when you wake up in the morning. Will you drag yourself out of bed and start the day by complaining? Or are you ready to say *next* and make that first step in the morning a step towards a new direction in life? Can you make the conscious decision to change your *fate* and ultimately your *destiny* by changing your attitude about life? Believe me when I say that you will experience a better life and become an even better person when you *next* life's everyday situations. Start right now. Just say *"I'm going to take that next step to a better life"* and then begin the process of making changes in your life.

THE END OF OUR MEETING

This chapter concludes our little meeting. We sat down together in chapter one to explore how *next* and *next step* could change your *fate* and *destiny*. We talked about developing a *go for it* attitude and the skills necessary to *make it happen* in many of life's situation. We have reviewed some of life's experiences, both my own and others, and I hope you picked up some ideas to help you along that never ending road we call life.

I am confident that the very next time you look in a mirror, the image looking back at you will be a real winner. Someone that is ready to take control of his or her life by constantly taking that *next step* in all of life's situations. I know you can do it and so do you. Go back through this book and re-read chapters that will help you to understand the necessity of always taking that *next step*.

What is of equal importance is that you realize that it will be *next* not "luck" that will bring positive changes in your life. Trying to win the lottery or waiting for some un-earned money to come your way will never bring the results you are really looking for. You and only you can make the type of changes in your life that will truly make you a better and happier person.

Remember, *It's A Great Life If You Don't Weaken* so don't get *weak* on yourself. Learn how to become a person of strong character. Be someone who knows who they are and where they are going in life, a person who knows right from wrong, good from bad and can always take that *next step* to a better and more fulfilling lifestyle.

Now comes the most important part of all. When you close this book, will you do something to change your *fate* and *destiny?* Or, are you going to continue going on with your life the way it is and has always been? There is no time better than right now for you to stand up and take that *NEXT STEP* to a new and exciting life. Go ahead, stand up and take your first *step* towards a new life and a new you. Set your mind towards only positive thinking, new changes in your life's direction and in no time at you will believe that ***It's A Great Life If You Don't Weaken.*** Now ***GO FOR IT and MAKE IT HAPPEN.***

Conclusion

If you have read this book from cover to cover and feel you understand some of my *next* philosophy, you are well on your way to a better understanding of yourself and life in general.

As author of this book, I found it a challenge to generalize the concepts of *Next* for the public at large. More importantly, I don't know each reader's level of understanding of life. Perhaps you have a great outlook on life and are extremely knowledgeable about your existence. You may have an understanding of life from both the scientific perspective as well as what it means to possess spiritual wisdom and universal knowledge. Then again, you may not have the foggiest idea of what that sentence means.

Irrespective of what your awareness of life may be, it is important that *you* understand that the black and white pages of this book represent my own personal viewpoint. This is my outlook on how someone can have a more enjoyable life. Not included in this book are numerous understandings of the totality of life itself, many of which I embrace. For you to truly grow as an individual, you need to understand your spirit and your purpose on earth. Research all the books and information available about your soul and spirit before you came to earth. Discover how to live a fulfilled life with an understanding that at some point in time your life on earth will be over. Explore the many ways you can obtain peace of mind about your life after death.

Depending on your age and knowledge of life to date, you owe it yourself to experience all that life has to offer. Learn why people have a dream catcher hanging over their bed. Find out why there are so many seminars and conventions on Whole Life Experiences. Look into the scientific and medical explanations of life and compare them with religious and ancient findings.

You did not come into being as a dog, cat, or any other form of life. You are a human being and possess greatness far beyond that of any other living thing. Don't take your life for granted. Embrace it. Enjoy every minute of it. Explore all that life has to offer. Believe me when I say *"there is so much to life that to ignore it means you will miss great opportunities and wonderful life changing events."* Events that can take you to heights you never dreamed possible. Don't let your time on earth go to waste. Take that *next step* right now and experience life in a way you could never imagine. Just tell yourself, *"NEXT*—I'm going to *GO FOR IT* and *MAKE IT HAPPEN."* Believe me, when you do that, it will change your life forever. After all, *It's A Great Life If You Don't Weaken.*

Jerry X. Shea

Attributes of a Weak & Strong personality

<u>WEAK</u>	<u>STRONG</u>
1. Does not believe in self	1. Believes in one's self
2. Unable to love others	2. Can give unconditional love
3. Needs others to love them	3. Loves themself for who they are
4. Must always be right	4. Willing to say "I'm wrong"
5. Claims their life it full of stress	5. What is stress anyway?
6. Never enough time	6. Manages time between family, work and pleasure
7. Dresses like a loser	7. Dresses like a winner
8. Hates holidays	8. Entertains on holidays
9. Will show up empty handed when invited to someone's home for dinner	9. Always brings a bottle of wine, box of candy or something as a gesture of appreciation for the dinner invitation
10. Eats without any concern for health	10. Eats healthy foods
11. Has no life goals	11. Sets goals for family, work and retirement
12. Spends family money on gambling – especially lottery tickets	12. Invests long term - saves for retirement
13. Thinks exercise is stupid	13. Has a cardiovascular exercise program

14. Smokes	14. Doesn't have a death wish
15. Ignores the obvious	15. Reacts to the obvious
16. Ignores the facts	16. Evaluates the facts
17. Lives only for today (Not to be confused with "living one day at a time" – AA motto)	17. Enjoys today with an eye on tomorrow
18. Skips elections, gripes about government	18. Exercises the right as a free American to cast a secret ballot at every election
19. Watches old reruns instead of the news	19. Watches the news and stays up with current events
20. Has no idea of what they spend each month	20. Lives within a monthly budget
21. Cannot balance a checkbook	21. Can balance their checkbook
22. Lives outside their means	22. Lives within their means
23. Do not pick up after themselves	23. Always pick up after after themselves
24. Watches thing happen	24. Makes things happen
25. Hates getting up in in the morning	25. Jumps out of bed to greet and embrace the day
26. Arrives at work 10 minutes late	26. Arrives at work 10 minutes early
27. Blames everyone else for their failure	27. Accepts their own failure
28. No self-discipline	28. Great self-discipline

29. Cannot accept defeat in a sports game

29. It's just a game – get over it

30. Has hard time giving a compliment

30. Can give a compliment in a truthful and tactful way

31. Jealous lover

31. Believes "Love is letting go"

32. Never brings home flowers

32. Without any special reason, will bring home flowers

33. Can't cook – eats out

33. Loves to cook – eats in

34. Would kick a dog if it got in the way

34. Would kick the person that that kicks that dog

35. Can't find anything nice to say about their in-laws

35. Accepts the in-laws for who they are and thankful for the son or daughter they married

36. Life sucks

36. Life is great

37. Job sucks

37. Happy to have a job

38. Hates others

38. Loves everyone

39. Hates animals

39. Loves animals

40. Is a bigot

40. Accepts everyone

41. Drinks to get drunk

41. Drinks responsibly

42. Drives drunk

42. Drives sober

43. Drives unsafe cars with bald tires

43. Values their family. Keeps the car tuned-up and good tires

44. Still lives at home

44. Left home after school

45. Can't talk to people

45. Learned how to talk to people

46. Gets defensive and responds quickly

46. Waits to cool down before responding

47. Only gives 80% and thinks it is 100%

47. Gives 100% and when asked will give 110%

48. Wants all the "thanks"

48. Gives thanks freely

49. Would sell out their folks or grandparents

49. Would never sell out anyone

50. These 50 are stupid

50. Understands these 50

Don't be so concerned about making a living
that you don't take the time to make a life.

About the Author

Jerry X Shea spent the early part of his life as a bio-medical photographer and cardiac technician dealing with life and death medical situations for heart patients. He also owned six small businesses over a forty year time span. Mr. Shea's insight into the daily struggles many of us face is what provided the basis for this book. From working in the health field to managing employees, dealing with vendors, landlords, customers, civic concerns, economic swings and a full family life have constantly reinforced Mr. Shea's *next* philosophy. His life stories are full of great examples of how *next* pertains to dealing with people, setting goals for yourself and enjoying a successful lifestyle.

Mr. Shea is an accomplished keynote speaker and a twenty year member of Toastmasters International. He is the author of *IT LOOKS EASY! IS IT? Simple Steps for Small Business Success* (ISBN 0-9712622-0-9) and *Prospecting, Presentation, Close* (ISBN 978-0-9712622-1-8). Both are published by his publishing company, Icon Holdings, Inc.

Mr. Shea and his wife Mary married in 1974 and moved to the small seaside tourist community of Cambria, California in 1999. Until 2007 they owned the Cambria Coffee Den Roasting Company and Pines by the Sea Properties, Inc.

With their home rented out long term they now travel the country in a large motorhome bringing Mr. Shea's lectures and workshops to towns along the way.

You can follow Mr. Shea's travels at the following link

www.jerryxshea,com

Resources, References, and Notes

Byrne, Robert , (November 1991). The 637 Best Things Anybody Ever Said. A Fawcett Crest Book Published by Ballantine Books, Sixteenth Printing

Collins, Williams - Language. World Publishing Co., Inc.

Coronary Atherosclerosis in Soldiers (July 18, 1953 - re-printed November 28, 1985). Journal of the American Medical Association.

Corsini, Raymond J. - Encyclopedia of Psychology. Published by John Wiley & Sons.

Goldenson, Robert M. PHD - Encyclopedia of Human Behavior – Psychology, Psychiatry, and Mental Health. Published by Doubleday & Company, Inc.

Lacey, A.R. A Dictionary of Philosophy. Department of Philosophy, King's College, University of London. Published by Routledge & Kegan Paul LTD. © A.R.Lacey 1976, 1986, 1996

Mautner, Thomas (edited by) - A Dictionary of Philosophy. Blackwell Reference

Merch, Sharp & Dohme Research Laboratories - The Merck Manual of Diagnosis and Therapy. Merck, Sharp, & Dohme.

Merriam-Webster's Collegiate Dictionary, Eleventh Edition, 2004

Pollan, Stephen M. & Levine, Mark - Die Broke - A Radical, Four-Part Financial Plan. HarperCollins Publishers, Inc.

Shaw, Harry - Dictionary of Literary Terms. McGraw-Hill Book Company

Zera, Richard S. - 1001 Quips & Quotes for Business Speeches. Published by Sterling Publishing Company, Inc. New York, N.Y.